Interest Groups in the Canadian Federal System

This is Volume 69 in the series of studies commissioned as part of the research program of the Royal Commission on the Economic Union and Development Prospects for Canada.

This volume reflects the views of the author and does not imply endorsement by the Chairman or Commissioners.

Interest Groups in the Canadian Federal System

HUGH G. THORBURN

Published by the University of Toronto Press in cooperation with the Royal Commission on the Economic Union and Development Prospects for Canada and the Canadian Government Publishing Centre, Supply and Services Canada

University of Toronto Press
Toronto   Buffalo   London

Grateful acknowledgment is made to the following for permission to reprint previously published and unpublished material: Methuen Publications; McGraw-Hill Ryerson Limited.

© Minister of Supply and Services Canada 1985

Printed in Canada
ISBN 0-8020-7317-4 ISSN 0829-2396
Cat. No. Z1-1983/1-41-69E

CANADIAN CATALOGUING IN PUBLICATION DATA

Main entry under title:
Thorburn, Hugh G., 1924 –
Interest groups in the Canadian federal system

(*The Collected research studies / Royal Commission on the Economic Union and Development Prospects for Canada.*
ISSN 0829-2396 ; 69)
Includes bibliographical references.
ISBN 0-8020-7317-4

1. Pressure groups – Canada. 2. Federal-provincial relations – Canada. 3. Federal government – Canada. I. Royal Commission on the Economic Union and Development Prospects for Canada. II. Title. III. Series: Research studies (Royal Commission on the Economic Union and Development Prospects for Canada); 69.

JL148.5T48 1985   322.4'3'0971   C85-099117-X

PUBLISHING COORDINATION: Ampersand Communications Services Inc.
COVER DESIGN: Will Rueter
INTERIOR DESIGN: Brant Cowie/Artplus Limited

CONTENTS

FOREWORD

When the members of the Rowell-Sirois Commission began their collective task in 1937, very little was known about the evolution of the Canadian economy. What was known, moreover, had not been extensively analyzed by the slender cadre of social scientists of the day.

When we set out upon our task nearly 50 years later, we enjoyed a substantial advantage over our predecessors; we had a wealth of information. We inherited the work of scholars at universities across Canada and we had the benefit of the work of experts from private research institutes and publicly sponsored organizations such as the Ontario Economic Council and the Economic Council of Canada. Although there were still important gaps, our problem was not a shortage of information; it was to interrelate and integrate — to synthesize — the results of much of the information we already had.

The mandate of this Commission is unusually broad. It encompasses many of the fundamental policy issues expected to confront the people of Canada and their governments for the next several decades. The nature of the mandate also identified, in advance, the subject matter for much of the research and suggested the scope of enquiry and the need for vigorous efforts to interrelate and integrate the research disciplines. The resulting research program, therefore, is particularly noteworthy in three respects: along with original research studies, it includes survey papers which synthesize work already done in specialized fields; it avoids duplication of work which, in the judgment of the Canadian research community, has already been well done; and, considered as a whole, it is the most thorough examination of the Canadian economic, political and legal systems ever undertaken by an independent agency.

The Commission's Research Program was carried out under the joint direction of three prominent and highly respected Canadian scholars: Dr. Ivan Bernier (*Law and Constitutional Issues*), Dr. Alan Cairns (*Politics and Institutions of Government*) and Dr. David C. Smith (*Economics*).

Dr. Ivan Bernier is Dean of the Faculty of Law at Laval University. Dr. Alan Cairns is former Head of the Department of Political Science at the University of British Columbia and, prior to joining the Commission, was William Lyon Mackenzie King Visiting Professor of Canadian Studies at Harvard University. Dr. David C. Smith, former Head of the Department of Economics at Queen's University in Kingston, is now Principal of that University. When Dr. Smith assumed his new responsibilities at Queen's in September, 1984, he was succeeded by Dr. Kenneth Norrie of the University of Alberta and John Sargent of the federal Department of Finance, who together acted as co-directors of Research for the concluding phase of the Economics research program.

I am confident that the efforts of the Research Directors, research coordinators and authors whose work appears in this and other volumes, have provided the community of Canadian scholars and policy makers with a series of publications that will continue to be of value for many years to come. And I hope that the value of the research program to Canadian scholarship will be enhanced by the fact that Commission research is being made available to interested readers in both English and French.

I extend my personal thanks, and that of my fellow Commissioners, to the Research Directors and those immediately associated with them in the Commission's research program. I also want to thank the members of the many research advisory groups whose counsel contributed so substantially to this undertaking.

DONALD S. MACDONALD

At its most general level, the Royal Commission's research program has examined how the Canadian political economy can better adapt to change. As a basis of enquiry, this question reflects our belief that the future will always take us partly by surprise. Our political, legal and economic institutions should therefore be flexible enough to accommodate surprises and yet solid enough to ensure that they help us meet our future goals. This theme of an adaptive political economy led us to explore the interdependencies between political, legal and economic systems and drew our research efforts in an interdisciplinary direction.

The sheer magnitude of the research output (more than 280 separate studies in 72 volumes) as well as its disciplinary and ideological diversity have, however, made complete integration impossible and, we have concluded, undesirable. The research output as a whole brings varying perspectives and methodologies to the study of common problems and we therefore urge readers to look beyond their particular field of interest and to explore topics across disciplines.

The three research areas, *Law and Constitutional Issues*, under Ivan Bernier, *Politics and Institutions of Government* under Alan Cairns, and *Economics* under David C. Smith (co-directed with Kenneth Norrie and John Sargent for the concluding phase of the research program) — were further divided into 19 sections headed by research coordinators.

The area *Law and Constitutional Issues* has been organized into five major sections headed by the research coordinators identified below.

- Law, Society and the Economy — *Ivan Bernier and Andrée Lajoie*
- The International Legal Environment — *John J. Quinn*
- The Canadian Economic Union — *Mark Krasnick*
- Harmonization of Laws in Canada — *Ronald C.C. Cuming*
- Institutional and Constitutional Arrangements — *Clare F. Beckton and A. Wayne MacKay*

Since law in its numerous manifestations is the most fundamental means of implementing state policy, it was necessary to investigate how and when law could be mobilized most effectively to address the problems raised by the Commission's mandate. Adopting a broad perspective, researchers examined Canada's legal system from the standpoint of how law evolves as a result of social, economic and political changes and how, in turn, law brings about changes in our social, economic and political conduct.

Within *Politics and Institutions of Government*, research has been organized into seven major sections.

- Canada and the International Political Economy — *Denis Stairs and Gilbert Winham*
- State and Society in the Modern Era — *Keith Banting*
- Constitutionalism, Citizenship and Society — *Alan Cairns and Cynthia Williams*
- The Politics of Canadian Federalism — *Richard Simeon*
- Representative Institutions — *Peter Aucoin*
- The Politics of Economic Policy — *G. Bruce Doern*
- Industrial Policy — *André Blais*

This area examines a number of developments which have led Canadians to question their ability to govern themselves wisely and effectively. Many of these developments are not unique to Canada and a number of comparative studies canvass and assess how others have coped with similar problems. Within the context of the Canadian heritage of parliamentary government, federalism, a mixed economy, and a bilingual and multicultural society, the research also explores ways of rearranging the relationships of power and influence among institutions to restore and enhance the fundamental democratic principles of representativeness, responsiveness and accountability.

Economics research was organized into seven major sections.

- Macroeconomics — *John Sargent*
- Federalism and the Economic Union — *Kenneth Norrie*
- Industrial Structure — *Donald G. McFetridge*
- International Trade — *John Whalley*
- Income Distribution and Economic Security — *François Vaillancourt*
- Labour Markets and Labour Relations — *Craig Riddell*
- Economic Ideas and Social Issues — *David Laidler*

Economics research examines the allocation of Canada's human and other resources, how institutions and policies affect this allocation, and the distribution of the gains from their use. It also considers the nature of economic development, the forces that shape our regional and industrial structure, and our economic interdependence with other countries. The thrust of the research in economics is to increase our comprehension of what determines our economic potential and how instruments of economic policy may move us closer to our future goals.

One section from each of the three research areas — The Canadian Economic Union, The Politics of Canadian Federalism, and Federalism and the Economic Union — have been blended into one unified research effort. Consequently, the volumes on Federalism and the Economic Union as well as the volume on The North are the results of an interdisciplinary research effort.

We owe a special debt to the research coordinators. Not only did they organize, assemble and analyze the many research studies and combine their major findings in overviews, but they also made substantial contributions to the Final Report. We wish to thank them for their performance, often under heavy pressure.

Unfortunately, space does not permit us to thank all members of the Commission staff individually. However, we are particularly grateful to the Chairman, The Hon. Donald S. Macdonald, the Commission's Executive Director, Gerald Godsoe, and the Director of Policy, Alan Nymark, all of whom were closely involved with the Research Program and played key roles in the contribution of Research to the Final Report. We wish to express our appreciation to the Commission's Administrative Advisor, Harry Stewart, for his guidance and advice, and to the Director of Publishing, Ed Matheson, who managed the research publication process. A special thanks to Jamie Benidickson, Policy Coordinator and Special Assistant to the Chairman, who played a valuable liaison role between Research and the Chairman and Commissioners. We are also grateful to our office administrator, Donna Stebbing, and to our secretarial staff, Monique Carpentier, Barbara Cowtan, Tina DeLuca, Françoise Guilbault and Marilyn Sheldon.

Finally, a well deserved thank you to our closest assistants, Jacques J.M. Shore, *Law and Constitutional Issues*; Cynthia Williams and her successor Karen Jackson, *Politics and Institutions of Government*; and I. Lilla Connidis, *Economics*. We appreciate not only their individual contribution to each research area, but also their cooperative contribution to the research program and the Commission.

IVAN BERNIER
ALAN CAIRNS
DAVID C. SMITH

PREFACE

Policy making in many advanced western countries, it is often said, revolves around bargaining between government and the major organized interest groups in society: business, labour and agriculture. Policy making in Canada, it is even more often argued, revolves around bargaining between federal and provincial governments. How are these two areas — one based on public-private interaction, one on government-government relationships — to be integrated? How does federalism affect the distribution of power among various private interests? How does it structure the ways these interests seek to influence governments? And how does the activity of organized interest groups shape and modify the way in which the federal system works?

These are some of the questions addressed by Professor Hugh Thorburn, a Queen's University political scientist, in his research study for the Commission. He first casts a wide net, exploring the literature linking the various levels of government with the economic interests of different groupings in the evolution of the federal system. Then he examines differing views concerning the contemporary impact of federalism on interest groups: Does the focus on the territorial issues of federalism divert attention from the more substantive non-territorial interests articulated by groups? Does the territorial division of power in our political system create fragmented, and perhaps weakened, interest groups? Do federalism and provincial barriers to the economic union frustrate the operations of interests that operate across the whole Canadian market? Which is the more accurate image — of interest groups ground between the millstones of competing governments . . . or of interests benefiting from the multiple access points that federalism offers?

Interest group perceptions of the virtues and disadvantages of federalism have seldom been systematically explored. Professor Thorburn takes advantage of the more than one thousand briefs submitted to the Royal

Commission on the Economic Union and Development Prospects for Canada, examining how private interests — groups, individuals and forums — view the operations of the federal system. He finds that few call for substantial shifts in governmental responsibilities, but that many call for improved federal-provincial coordination, for reductions in overlapping and duplication, and for reduced federal-provincial conflict. Professor Thorburn concludes by asking how we can better integrate the two vital and equally necessary processes of intergovernmental consultation and government–private interest consultation within the framework of institutional reforms. His work offers a fresh and much needed perspective on the implications of federalism for Canadian policy and society.

RICHARD SIMEON

ACKNOWLEDGMENTS

To be useful for the Commission, this report on the interrelations of the federal system and the interest group system in Canada had to be submitted about seven months after my contract was signed. The area is a large one, and the interrelations of the two dynamics are largely unexplored in earlier work. The sources for the study were basically two: the substantial literature that already exists on Canadian federalism and that on interest groups, plus the briefs to the Commission (most of which are from interest groups or business representatives). To cope with these extensive sources in such a short time period I turned to others for help. Carol Reardon and Lison Fougère prepared reports on the existing literature.

To cope with the voluminous submissions to the Commission, I was permitted access to all briefs and transcripts and to the analysis that the staff was preparing: tables classifying the material, and "content analysis" — in this case excerpts of key statements from the interventions by groups and individuals. Jacques Bérard of the Commission secretariat staff prepared a preliminary report of the interventions. I am especially grateful for the assistance of Bruce Pollard, who integrated the tabular and content analysis material for Chapter 5.

Thomas Hueglin was extremely helpful in assisting with the last chapter, especially the discussion of interorganizational decision making. Leisa McDonald typed all drafts and the final copy.

I express thanks to all of these people for their help and inspiration. They made it possible for the study to be presented almost on time. The responsibility for faults and shortcomings must be mine, but I insist on sharing it with the shortness of time.

Finally, I wish to thank Richard Simeon, the coordinator of this and other studies on the federal system. He was generous with his time and offered a balance between contributions of ideas and approaches, which were always stimulating and realistic, and a firm insistence on meeting commitments. The result produced good conditions for research: stimulation, pace and structure.

H.G.T.

December 1984

Introduction

Canada, like other industrial democracies, has developed a pattern of organized interest groups competing to influence government policy. Given the pressure on the public treasury traceable to the current state of economic stagnation, the governments (provincial and federal) are forced to exercise great selectivity in choosing among distributive policies and stimulative initiatives. Increasing financial stringency, combined with the growing demands of organized interests for assistance and of political parties reflecting pressing public expectations for government action, have created a problem of governability for Canada, as for other Western democracies.

Federalism adds a further dimension to the problem by involving the country in two separate yet interdependent levels of government, each with its own party and interest group system; these governments then develop a complex pattern of interaction among themselves. This complex decision-making structure is often rightly considered a contributing cause of the country's indifferent economic performance in recent years. Provincial governments are expected to act in the interest of their citizens, and this can produce policies that assail the country's economic union. At the same time there is a general perception among Canadians that federal-provincial conflict should be curbed, in favour of a more consensual approach to mutual problem-solving, especially in the area of economic policy.

However, as we shall see, much of the basis for the conflict is to be found in the regional segmentation and asymmetry of the national economy itself. Industry is mainly concentrated in Central Canada, and the resource industries are scattered over the vast territories of the world's second-largest country. Quebec is a special case as a French-speaking province with a definite will to defend the socio-cultural interests of its people as well as its industry, which is less developed than that of Ontario but more so than that of the outlying provinces. The economic interest groups often relate more to one level of government than the other (e.g., finance and transportation to the federal level, and the resource industries and small business to the provincial). The high level of foreign ownership of industry has served to integrate key Canadian industries into a North American economic system, which in turn has encouraged even more foreign ownership and control. This has helped to undermine the traditional east-west economy that was the objective of Confederation and the National Policy.

The above summary describes a situation that is serious. If it is correct, there is need for basic institutional or structural reform. However, when we examine the briefs to the Commission, especially those from business, the tone is much more complacent. The message, generally, is that there is little really wrong with Canada's institutions and practices that could not be put right by government leaving the market to do its job. Government should be a facilitator, not an active participant in economic life. Perhaps this situation reveals that business is fairly content with its relationship with government, which treats it as a privileged adviser. Or, perhaps Canadian interest groups are not fully aware of the economic advantages being attained in other countries from certain kinds of governmental actions.

This report seeks to explain and clarify the development of interests since Confederation in 1867 and to analyze their relations with the two orders of government in current experience. How does the axis of government-interest group relations relate to that of the intergovernmental relations of the federal system? In which ways are the two axes crosscutting? And how do they reinforce each other?

Finally, some suggestions are put forward for integrating the two processes so that they can support a better structure of policy making, especially in economic affairs. The objective is to work out a means for structuring the mechanisms of political bargaining so that they produce a higher level of interest harmonization and coordination. In this perspective, the interest group system and the intergovernmental system should, if possible, be helped to strengthen and support one another.

Chapter 1

The Focus of the Study:
Two Overlapping Dynamics

Policy making in Canadian government is dominated by two separate processes of consultation and negotiation: one between private interest groups and individual governments, and a second between governments themselves — federal to provincial and, less frequently, provincial to provincial. Each of these is separately examined.

The Dynamic of Interest Group Consultation

Canada had its beginnings in a situation of close relationships between private interest groups and the colonial governments. In the United Province of Canada, before Confederation, commercial capitalist interests sponsored the development of railways and canals, which formed the infrastructure for the developing colony. A desire to expand the horizons of the colonies west into the Prairies and east to the Maritimes, combined with fear of the United States after the Civil War, were major incentives for the enlargement of the colonies into the new Dominion of Canada via Confederation. Representatives for such interests as the major banks, railways, shipping interests and trading companies had, from the very beginning, ongoing relations with the governments in British North America. Policy making was shared between these people and the elected politicians sitting in the cabinets of Canada and the provinces. Therefore, the pattern of what was later known as elite accommodation, or pressure group politics, was a thriving arrangement from the very beginnings of Canada's history as a nation. Governments were closely involved in the financing and planning of railways and other major projects of development. Connections were forged between these capitalist interests and the political party leaders of Canada, and through them with the governments, provincial and federal. Such well known events as the Pacific Scandal in the 1870s bear witness to the close collaborative or patronage arrangements that existed at that time.

With the passage of time, the relatively informal personal relations that developed between leading politicians and their higher civil servants, on the one hand, and the business leaders, on the other, hardened into a more bureaucratic relationship. As governments built up larger administrative structures in order to deliver services to the community, interest groups in the areas of activity that were closest in relation to these governmental initiatives were called into being. Close clientele relations developed between individual departments of government and the communities they served, typified by the close collaboration existing between the Canadian Federation of Agriculture and the federal and provincial departments of agriculture. Similar relationships developed in other major sectors, such as forestry, mining and secondary manufacturing. Policies relating to the support of these industries and their protection through tariffs and import regulations of various kinds were elaborated through consultation by government representatives with the spokesmen for these substantial interests. Relations with other major concentrations of capital in such institutions as the banks, insurance companies, railways and grain trading companies were established with governments in order to influence policy as it affected individual private concerns.

Businesses saw the advantage of organizing associations, permitting them to collaborate in their consultation with governments. Permanent organizations with specialist staff were built up to carry on liaison with government in the most propitious manner possible.

These representations were carried on not only with government leaders, such as ministers and their senior civil service associates, but also extended to committees of Parliament and the provincial legislatures and often involved representations to private members of Parliament, both on government and opposition sides. It was generally conceded that the groups had a right to be heard before policy affecting them was finalized by either order of government, provincial or federal.

Communities of interest developed, composed of politicians, bureaucrats and interest group representatives organized along functional lines. Associations, some pan-Canadian, some regional or local, each devoted to advancing the substantive concerns of its members, worked together where their interests coincided, and in opposition to one another when they diverged. Their concern was to influence policy along with other matters: legislation, the formulation of regulations, day-to-day administration and the general attitudes of government. Government came to rely for information upon these groups as a major input in the policy-making process. Their relationship, therefore, was not an adversarial one but one of collaboration in a common enterprise. The support of the groups could at times extend beyond the supply of information and advice to other considerations affecting the well-being of the political parties and personalities concerned.

The result was a kind of parallel process in government. On the one hand, there was the representative system which saw members of Parliament elected in their constituencies to sit in the legislative assemblies and hold the government responsible. While legislation was usually government initiated, the majority party would have to give its assent if it was to be enacted. The opposition soon developed the habit of systematic criticism of and at times obstruction to these initiatives. The dynamics of the system involved a continuous campaign by the opposition to show up the inadequacies of the government, and a corresponding attempt by government members, under cabinet leadership, to show up the opposition as incompetent, irresponsible and ill-informed. The electors were called upon at fairly regular intervals of about four years to decide which side would form the government in the ensuing period.

Parallel to this was the government to private interest relationship, which was much less widely known but was nonetheless important. Through this arrangement, advice, supplemented by at times considerable pressure, was focussed upon the government to induce it to adopt the policies favoured by individual groups. The government, therefore, was subjected to these two processes of advice and pressure, and it had to make its way between them. At times the representations would be parallel and consistent; at other times they would go in two or more directions, and the government would either have to reconcile the various positions in some kind of compromise or make hard choices between them. The task of the government then was a more difficult and complex one than appeared to the casual eye of the citizen, who was much more aware of the representative, official structures than of the more informal and less conspicuous interest group process.

Interest groups began to receive serious scholarly attention in the mid-1960s, and since that time the body of interest group literature has grown. Most of this work, however, is made up of case studies, with very little theoretical work to support it.

Most definitions of interest groups stress the link between a socially based interest and the attempt to influence public policy. David Truman's oft-cited definition saw interest groups as a "shared attitude group that makes certain claims through or upon other groups in society. . . . If and when it makes its claims through or upon any of the institutions of government, it becomes a political interest group" (Truman, 1951, p. 37). A more useful definition for analytical purposes is provided by A. Paul Pross: "Interest groups are organizations whose members act together to influence public policy in order to promote their common interest" (Pross, 1975b, p. 2).

The major concern of political scientists has been with the extent of these groups' influence over government policy making. This "communication function" is determined by the structure of the group, the functioning of the group and its access to government. Structure refers to the degree of organizational sophistication. A group that is highly institutionalized will possess the resources to establish a permanent staff that can seek to influence government on a continual basis and offer advice on a wide variety of issues. On the other hand, groups with only loose and volatile structures are more likely to have to resort to public confrontational approaches. This is the case especially for issue-oriented groups. This approach helps to compensate for small and fluctuating memberships.

Interest groups provide a forum where their members can compare and exchange information about common problems and about the effects of proposed government action or changing social conditions. Shared attitudes emerge about the suitability of various government actions and the need to influence government in these directions (Zukowsky, n.d., p. 10). Finally, a precondition of influence is the communication of these shared attitudes to the appropriate decision makers. Therefore, securing access is a vital part of exercising influence on government. Access can occur at a number of points in the political system: the bureaucracy, the cabinet, members of Parliament, and officials of political parties. Not all access points are valued equally, but groups will try to maintain as many contacts as their resources will allow.

Access alone will not ensure that a group will be successful in influencing government. The communication of group concerns is of little impact unless decision makers can be induced to accept the interest group recommendations and support them. For their part, governments have two primary interests in pressure groups. They value the information that groups are able to provide, and they seek out the legitimacy that interest group support can give to their policies. Continued access to the centre of power depends on the degree to which a group can fulfill these needs reliably and well. The size of the membership, the control of financial resources, the monopoly of technical knowledge, the prestige of the groups' leaders and the willingness of the group to cooperate and avoid outright confrontation are important elements in gaining recognized status within government (Schwartz, 1978, p. 331). David Kwavnick observes that within the labour movement, the competition for recognition from government is at least as important to the major labour unions in Canada as defending the immediate interests of their members (Kwavnick, 1970). This process has led some analysts to conclude that groups closely involved with government eventually become dependent on the state:

> Group involvement in the policy discussions not only expands the range of information available to government — it can be used to neutralize group objections to proposed legislation and to engage support for it. Government thus finds in the pressure group system a device for testing policy proposals and a means of eliciting support for them. (Pross, 1975b, p. 6)

This close relationship, according to Pross, can enhance the position of cooperative groups since they are guaranteed a measure of collaborative influence over policy decisions that affect their interests, but the groups must be willing to accept short-term defeats for continuing favourable relations in the long run. Appeals to Parliament, especially the opposition, or to the public at large, could jeopardize their privileged position with government. This arrangement may also serve the important function of keeping the political system abreast of changes within the social system, thereby promoting political stability:

> The successful performance of this last function, however, will depend on the sensitivity of the governmental and pressure group sub-systems to changes in their own immediate environments. Closed and captive agencies and groups through their failure to absorb external demands, may compound rigidities existing elsewhere in the system.　　　　　　　　(ibid., p. 7)

Pross offers a useful conceptual approach to understanding the role of interest groups in the political system. He ranges them on a continuum from institutionalized groups to issue-oriented ones. The underlying assumption of this approach is that "the organizational characteristics of a given group may have a great deal to do with the extent to which it performs recognized functions" (Pross 1976, pp. 132–33). His model incorporates the interrelationship between the structure and functioning of a group.

Institutional groups are:

> Groups that possess organizational continuity and cohesion, commensurate human and financial resources, extensive knowledge of those sectors of government that affect them and their clients, stable memberships, concrete and immediate operational objectives that are broad enough to permit each group to bargain with government over the application of specific legislation or the achievement of particular concessions, and a willingness to put organizational imperatives ahead of any particular policy concerns.　　　(ibid., p. 133)

Issued-oriented groups, as one would expect, have the reverse characteristics:

> Groups whose primary orientation is to issues, rather than to organizational continuity and cohesion; minimal and often naïve knowledge of government; fluid membership; a tendency to encounter difficulty in formulating and adhering to short-range objectives; a generally low regard for the organizational mechanisms they have developed for carrying out their goals; and, most important, a narrowly defined purpose, usually the resolution of one or two issues or problems, that inhibits the development of "selective inducements" designed to broaden the group's membership base.　　　(ibid.)

The implication of this approach is that the

> . . . capacity to act in pressure group politics is determined by the interaction of large-scale political forces and the internal characteristics of individual

groups. That is, the nature of the policy process in a given political system, its political culture, power structure, and so on define the general conditions of pressure group behaviour, but the actions of a specific group depends on the group's capacity to utilize internal resources.   (ibid.)

The advantage of the organizational base model is that it allows us to compare how different groups respond to different environments and to relate this behaviour to the structures and process of the policy system. At the theoretical level, the model shows that institutionalized groups have the financial and human resources necessary to participate in a system that encourages sustained collaboration between government agencies and their "recognized" client groups; on the other hand, issue-oriented groups can be effective in a competitive and open decision-making situation in which they can compensate for their insignificant size and lack of cohesion by rallying public opinion behind them. Their weak organizational base and narrow scope make them less valuable to governments as a steady and reliable source of information and legitimation, but they do serve an important warning function in any political system:

> In general systemic terms, issue-oriented groups enhance the adaptive capacity of the overall system, permitting a responsiveness to emergent issues that is not easily achieved by more cumbersome mechanisms of political communication. . . . Their chief advantage lies in their flexibility. Because they develop extremely quickly and are unencumbered by institutionalized structures, they are excellent vehicles for generating immediate public reaction to specific issues. Because their stake in the future is usually limited, they can indulge in forms of political communication that institutional groups are reluctant to use. This is particularly true in Canada where established groups tend not to resort to publicity for fear of disturbing relations with administrative agencies.
> (Pross, 1975b, p. 12)

In this sense, issue-oriented groups can act as a social barometer which forces decision makers to recognize the legitimacy of socially divisive issues that would otherwise be neglected. For example, the present increased political willingness to address the problem of drinking when driving is primarily due to the public concern generated by the efforts of the families of accident victims.

Pross's model can also be employed to analyze how the relationships between interest groups and government change over time. For example, a shift from a closed and secretive political system to one that is open and competitive would enhance the organizational advantages of issue-oriented groups. This, in fact, appears to be happening in Canada (as well as other Western countries) since the 1970s.

Prior to 1975, writing on Canadian pressure group politics demonstrates a general acceptance of the elite accommodation model as an accurate and complete description of pressure group behaviour. Essentially, this model posits a system of mutual accommodation between government and interest groups, in which social and economic elites alone determine the interest of society in informal, secretive, face-to-face contact between the upper echelons of government (ministers and their bureaucracies) and interest groups. Robert Presthus describes the Canadian political process as one in which "political leaders, including the senior bureaucracy, could and did define and seek the public interest without much need for explanation of their actions or for participation by the general public" (Presthus, 1971, p. 446). Pross attributes this situation to two main factors: (1) the closed, hierarchical nature of Canadian political structures, especially the bureaucracy and the party system; and (2) the limited extent to which the Canadian political system is based on a pluralistic, competitive approach to decision making:

> Some competition exists, of course — intergovernment rivalry arises out of the current exercise of power or the unclear definitions of jurisdiction — but within each government there is relatively little of the functional rivalry which typifies inter-agency competition in the United States. Similarly, the fact that the executive operates within a cabinet and parliamentary system of government means that rivalries between legislators cannot be readily exploited.
>
> (Pross, 1975b, pp. 18–19)

As a result, access to key decision makers has played a more important role in interest group activity than popularizing issues:

> The Canadian political system, then, tends to favour elite groups, making functional accommodative, consensus-seeking techniques of political communication, rather than conflict-oriented techniques that are directed towards the achievement of objectives through arousing public opinion.
>
> (ibid., p. 19)

Obviously, such a system of decision making strongly favours institutionalized groups over issue-oriented ones. Presthus outlines the most significant features of elite accommodation: (1) a built-in disposition toward support of the status quo because it restricts meaningful participation to established groups with a direct substantive interest in the process; (2) the tendency to define problems as essentially technical with the implication that political considerations are illegitimate and certainly divisive (the result is the uncoordinated incremental expansion of governmental and private programs without adequate direction by government); and (3) the crystallization of existing patterns of resource allocation, "which makes the introduction of new scientific, technical and economic directions difficult as they strike against established influence structures, based largely on long-standing, functionally determined, agency-clientele relationships" (Presthus, 1975, p. 351).

James Gillies argues that a relationship of mutual accommodation, where business and government worked together to plan the economy, was facilitated during the 1940s, 1950s and 1960s by their shared belief in how the goals of society (i.e., economic growth and prosperity) could be achieved. Since World War II, the issue-by-issue approach has been the most frequent strategy used by business to influence government. This approach is one in which:

> . . . business reacts to individual initiatives of the government as those initiatives are introduced. The ones that are perceived to be detrimental to the corporation or an industry — and the public interest — are opposed. It implies no grand strategy; it is simply, as it states, an approach that calls for dealing with issues as they develop. (Gillies, 1981, p. 48)

This approach rests on three major assumptions: first, that a close interrelationship with the bureaucracy, the executive and the legislature is the most effective means of influencing government and preventing the formulation of policies that are hostile to the interests of business:

> Indeed, trade association officials stress that one of their major duties is to keep close to the members of the bureaucracy so that they may spot the early evolution of ideas and inform their members about any developments that may influence their activities. (ibid.)

Second, it assumes policy flows from the bottom up and that the transmission of appropriate and useful information will stop an inappropriate policy from being enacted. Finally, it assumes that government accords business a special, privileged position over other interests, and therefore that the exercise of persuasion is a sufficient instrument for achieving its policy goals.

During the 1940s and 1950s, elite accommodation was facilitated by the growth of the bureaucratic state. Politicians took an incremental approach to the expansion of government activity after the Second World War; so responsibility for the planning and implementation of the massive intervention of the state was mainly left to the experts within the line departments. Government expansion occurred in an incremental, uncoordinated fashion, as each of the government agencies distributed resources according to its own professional norms. Therefore, the most important groups during this period were special interest groups whose concerns corresponded to the functions of separate government agencies. The special interest groups could offer officials the expertise and information necessary for the development of policy initiatives in return for policy input. Because most shared the same professional values as the government officials, cosy "clientele" relationships developed, where groups and government officials mutually agreed upon the appropriate form of action.

Despite this fundamental change in the role of the state in society, the policy-making structures of government remained relatively uncomplicated and informal:

> There were no committees of cabinet, except for the Treasury Board which was established by statute, and individual ministers operated in a highly independent manner. Any coordination that had to be undertaken was handled

by deputy ministers in a very informal fashion and in those days of less complex government, the system worked effectively. Individual ministers were powerful and ran the departments without advice, let alone interference from anyone. (Gillies and Pigott, 1982, p. 261)

Strong ministers such as C.D. Howe worked with their constituencies (in Howe's case the industrial community) and developed policies in collaboration with the groups and, it was assumed, in the interests of the country. No conflict was perceived between the private and the public interest. However, by the end of the 1960s, broad social changes and the continued growth of government led to a fundamental rebuilding of the policy-making structures at the federal level and in some of the provinces.

Pross cites three factors as the source of the emergent pattern in which institutionalized groups are "exposed to heightened public scrutiny and are more dependent on public opinion": (1) changes in the government policy-making structure designed to bring about central control over policy making; (2) the proliferation of interest groups, especially citizens' groups, in response to the growth of government and the increased exposure of the activities of institutionalized groups; and (3) the advent of television, which allowed groups to mobilize public support for their cause (Pross, 1975a, pp. 132–33)

Changes in the policy making structure began on a small scale in the early 1960s as governments became dissatisfied with the lack of political control over the growth of their expenditures and activities. However, the major restructuring of the system came after 1968, when Prime Minister Trudeau introduced a centralized cabinet committee system as a means of directing policy making within the cabinet as a whole. Hugh Faulkner observes that these structural changes give the appearance that ultimate power is highly concentrated within the policy process when, in practice, it is highly dispersed. One reason for this is that policy making from its earliest stages now involves coordination between a number of departments:

The new policy and expenditure management system . . . ensures that ministers must process any initiative that involves expenditures (which includes tax expenditures) through their cabinet colleagues. This process integrates policy decisions into the government priorities framework, tightens up decision-making by juxtaposing policy options and expenditures and strengthens the pattern of collegial authority over policy development and expenditure management. The effect is to limit the capacity of an individual minister to respond to interest groups. To take an initiative in one area means that another area is going to be affected. Trade-offs will be required, so that the other area has to be massaged as well. Consequently, interest groups must now be prepared to deal with the whole range of cabinet, including the cabinet committees, the membership of which has only recently become public information. (Faulkner, 1982, p. 243)

This, of course, spreads a group's resources even thinner than before, as more contacts are necessary to petition government effectively.

The problem for groups is compounded because the federal example was followed at the provincial level. Ontario and Quebec adopted the same type of committee structure a few years later, and the other provinces too made similar adjustments in their structures.

Perhaps more important than the cabinet committee system itself has been the concomitant growth and development of central agencies. The Privy Council Office and its close affiliate, the Federal-Provincial Relations Office, have become crucial to the policy-making process, having assumed responsibility for advising cabinet on the integration of policy recommendations into the general framework of government objectives. Gillies and Pigott argue that the shift in influence from departments to the central agencies of government has seriously affected the ability of established groups to penetrate the decision-making process. Despite the important policy-making role played by the Privy Council Office, its officials "simply do not see their function as dealing with individual legislative thrusts, but as coordinating various inputs into the policy-making process" (Gillies and Pigott, 1982, p. 262). While the traditional channels of involvement are no longer adequate:

> . . . special interests do not have a satisfactory method of inserting their input into the determination of the public interest in anything like as meaningful a fashion as was once the case. (ibid., p. 263)

Finally, the increased complexity of the policy-making process, due to the increasing speed and unpredictability of social and technological change, has meant that government has had to try to improve its mechanisms for interest group involvement and employ new techniques to facilitate the process. Since the 1970s, there has been a formalization of consultative devices, as the government attempted to augment its information coming from society to adapt to changing conditions. One such development was the increase in the use of white papers. Audrey D. Doerr observes that since the advent of the Trudeau administration, the white paper has been used by the federal government "to promote and stimulate broad public debate among interested groups and individuals, so that the government can receive direction from those people who will be most affected by the policies" (Doerr, 1971, p. 185). However, she notes that examples of public responses, by and large, represent the articulate and financially well-endowed sectors of the community which have an enhanced capacity to participate and perceive a sense of efficacy in participation (ibid., p. 197). Government has addressed this problem of underrepresentation with some success through financial assistance to groups with limited resources, such as welfare groups and consumer associations. The formalization of the process has had the twin advantages of opening-up the process to anyone determined enough to participate and, exposing who the vested interests are in a given policy area by making them operate through public structures.

This development of central agencies has been paralleled by similar arrangements at the provincial level, especially in Quebec and Ontario. Also, coloured papers (white papers, green papers, etc.) have been employed at that level to facilitate public discussion of policy issues with groups. This has, of course, greatly added to the burden of groups, just as it has increased their opportunities — opportunities more easily exploited by the larger and richer institutionalized groups.

A larger problem cited by Doerr is the lack of appropriate machinery to conduct debates with the general public. One promising step taken recently to improve this situation was the appointment of seven special parliamentary committees, or parliamentary task forces, which travelled the country providing early access to government policy proposals for the public, special interest groups and Parliament. Hugh Faulkner claims that the crucial issue in dealing with government overload is the absence of a legitimate process for defining the public interest in an ongoing manner, not the excessive control of big business. He considers the introduction of the parliamentary task force mechanism the most progressive change to date (Faulkner, 1982, p. 252).

A major consequence of these changes in consultative mechanisms is that groups are now expected to prepare formal presentations and to formulate detailed recommendations in a form that allows the government to compare the demands relating to government priorities of one group with those of another. All groups and individuals are now on a more equal footing in that greater emphasis is placed on the quality of group management, rather than on size or economic resources. This enhances the opportunities for smaller groups and individuals to participate in the policy-making process. As Faulkner, an ex-federal cabinet minister, has observed:

> . . . one of the ironies of the contemporary pressure group scene is that the influential interest groups today seem to be less satisfied with the results of their efforts than some of the less powerful. (ibid., p. 245)

The combined impact of the insularity of the Privy Council Office and the need for agencies and their associated interest groups to compete for scarce resources through open structures has forced institutionalized groups into the public arena and increased the public awareness of their activities. As a consequence, there has been a proliferation of citizens' groups established to counter the demands of vested interests. This has been especially true in those sections of the community that previously had no means of organization:

> . . . both agencies and groups discovered that by going public they have alerted other interests to the nature of the debates that are in progress and so have encouraged their participation and perhaps the formation of new groups. (Pross, 1982, p. 177)

In many cases, the formation of these groups has been facilitated by government funding.

In 1981 the Institute of Public Administration held a seminar on interest groups and government. As *rapporteur*, Paul Pross outlined the two schools of thought into which explanations for the proliferation of groups fall. There are those who support general environmental explanations, and those who argue that the expansion of group activities constitutes a "reactive spiral." The latter claim that the development of relations between groups and government has occurred incrementally and disjointedly and, in the process, has expanded both state activity and the constellation of formal groups which surround the state. Khayyam Paltiel, as reported by Pross, argued that:

> . . . the state itself is progenitor and prime mover in both the fostering of intervention and the formation of groups. Étatisme . . . is inspired from within the machinery of government, but must be buttressed and made legitimate by individuals and groups who are part of the general public. Hence the emergence of bureaucratic patronage and the fostering of supportive groups — to which other groups respond from a more traditional, individualistic ideological base. (ibid., p. 172)

Others attribute an active role to the state but steer clear of the *dirigiste* tendencies of Paltiel's explanation. Here the state is seen as fostering group activity in response to the public's expectation that certain groups should not be excluded from the process, rather than as a means of promoting support for its own initiatives. Women's groups and native groups, for example, are said to have been sponsored because government needed to hear from these sectors of the community before determining its policies.

These explanations are in many ways compatible with the environmentalist argument, which also views the proliferation of groups as an incremental response to both state activity and involvement of other pressure groups. The crucial difference is that environmentalists claim that the elaboration of government-group relations is not merely an extension of past relations but represents a fundamental change of the Canadian state into what is called the *dirigiste* state. Dominique Clift, in the same seminar, asserted that the Canadian state, now dominated by a "dynamic" public sector, co-opts what elements of the public it can and destroys those that oppose it. Clift describes it as a state in which "the kind of consensus that guides contemporary society comes not from the people, but is sponsored by the state itself" (cited in Pross, 1982, p. 181).

Paltiel's moderately *dirigiste* argument seems particularly persuasive. The need for government to deal with increasingly rapid and complex social change appears to have outdistanced the capacity of existing consultative mechanisms. As a result, there has been a tendency for such devices to become political tools for building the necessary support for decisions that have already been made by government. This is not entirely manipulative, for government may not always get the support it is looking for. However, as Doerr suggests, society will have to learn quickly if it is to participate meaningfully in policy formulation in the future (Doerr, 1971, p. 199).

A third factor that has influenced the environment within which pressure groups must now operate is the social impact of television. Television solved the problem of communication between interest groups and people in densely populated areas and gave groups the opportunity to mobilize a more general public reaction to political issues (Pross, 1976, p. 134). Issue-oriented groups have benefited most from this development; they have been able to compensate for their small and loosely organized membership by attracting public support. In fact, television can destabilize the position of established groups, which have always been able to rely for their strength on their firmly grounded status. Now established groups are compelled to cater to public opinion, as well as to the views of their membership in couching their demands. For example, Paul Pross commented:

> A.E. Diamond, president of the Canadian Institute of Public Real Estate Companies, recently offered an illustration of this process when he asserted that the CIPREC must "make the public more aware of the difficulties faced by developers" in order to challenge the power that various pressure groups have captured over the development process.　(Pross, 1975a, p. 127)

While television can focus public attention on an issue, it cannot act as a source of detailed demands. The complexity of most public policy and the resources needed to monitor the process mean that institutionalized groups are still in a better position to participate effectively in the complex structures of policy making. However, as indicated above, even institutionalized groups are experiencing great difficulty influencing government. Overall, a consequence of the recent changes in the policy-making environment of pressure groups seems to be an opening up of the process to greater public debate, though this has not necessarily been translated into policy outputs. There is reason to believe that this increased group activity masks the greater autonomy of the state to decide the course of government action.

The Dynamic of Federalism

Interest group relations in Canada are more complex than in many other countries, because Canada is a federal state in which the division of powers between the two levels of government leaves each level with considerable power, and the division is so constructed that many jurisdictional overlaps have developed. This problem was less serious in the nineteenth century than in more recent times, because with a simple primary economy, state activity generally was at a fairly low level then; and, therefore, the provincial and federal jurisdictions had little occasion to get in one another's way. However, with the development of the positive state in the twentieth century, both levels of government responded to a growing public demand for services and government supervisory and police activities, so that problems of coordination between the two levels of government grew.

The way the powers were distributed under the constitutional arrangements of 1867 invited serious problems of divided jurisdiction. The federal parliament was given control over trade and commerce between provinces and between Canada and foreign countries, while at the same time the provincial legislatures controlled this matter within their own borders — an invitation to jurisdictional conflict. The public lands were under provincial jurisdiction within their borders, which meant control over the natural resources of the country. On the other hand, the federal parliament had considerable powers over the regulation of business under the general grant of power to make laws for "the peace, order and good government of Canada," and also specifically to impose any form of taxes, to borrow money, and to control currency, coinage, banking, weights and measures, legal tender, bankruptcy, patents, copyrights, etc. In addition, it had jurisdiction over criminal law, which, of course, made it possible for it to declare certain activities to be crimes punishable under law. Also it had the residual power; i.e., all matters not assigned to the provincial legislatures belonged to the federal authority.

Over the years relations between the federal government and the provinces have changed. In the nineteenth century, governments, by modern standards, did very little, and what they did do was largely amply provided for in the distribution of powers without significant grounds for conflict. After all, the BNA Act (now the *Constitution Act, 1867*) was worked out by the Canadian politicians who would later have to make it function. They had given the control of the economy largely over to the federal government to permit the development of a commercial empire based on the St. Lawrence drainage basin and facilitated by a network of railways. On the other hand, to secure the assent of the French-Canadian clerical and bourgeois elite, the provinces had been assured control of those questions close to the concerns of the Church: education, social and charitable matters, faith and morals.[1]

However, with the shift from a largely rural, primary-producing economy to an urban, industrial one in the late nineteenth and early twentieth centuries, governments were soon drawn into enlarging their role to regulate and support the new industries and to protect the vulnerable urban work force that lacked the self-sufficiency and independence of the farmer-woodsman of the past. To do this, each level of government extended its activities so that it came into contact with the other level. Moreover, with the passage of time, new problems presented themselves that had not existed in 1867. They had to be dealt with — but by which level of government?

This is a complex story told and retold elsewhere. Suffice it here to say that the problems came to a head in the 1930s. The Depression challenged the governments profoundly and revealed a situation in which the provinces, after some sixty years of judicial interpretation of the Constitution, found their responsibility and powers enlarged from what they had been; yet there was no corresponding enlargement of their financial capacity to discharge these responsibilities. The federal government, therefore, had to step in by using its spending power to help out. The ground was laid for the somewhat unsatisfactory situation of today: overlapping jurisdictions and competing policy initiatives by the two levels of government.

This altered situation is related to the changes in the Canadian economy that have developed. Canada in the nineteenth and early twentieth centuries was largely an integrated country: the railways were the underpinning of an east-west economy. They carried primary products (wheat, lumber, etc.) to tidewater for export and took settlers and manufactures to the frontier to further development. The Canadian business elite orchestrated this development of nation-building.

After the First World War, the situation began to change, and by the 1950s it was completely transformed. The development of the new staples (base metals, pulp and paper, iron ore and, finally, petroleum) took place in relation to the U.S. market and was largely financed by U.S. capital. Also, the establishment of U.S. branch plants in Canada, producing American products for the Canadian market, further upset the east-west economy by superimposing a north-south one. Canada saw the earlier, integrating, reciprocal nation-building economy partially replaced by one that encouraged province-building. Under the newer arrangement each region developed its own north-south relations with its U.S. customers and entrepreneurial head offices, thereby attenuating its ties to Ottawa and the rest of Canada.

These pressures were bound to have their effects on Canadian federalism, reducing the salience of the federal government and enhancing that of the provinces. Since the latter controlled the public lands containing the natural resources, province-building was a natural outcome. But along with it came a complex cooperative relationship beteen the two levels of government.

Since all of these matters were bound to be of great interest to business-oriented interest groups, the situation invited their intervention at both levels of government to encourage courses of action that they found to be in their interest.

Relations Between the Dynamic
of Interest Group Consultation
and the Dynamic of Federalism

The two processes described above are very different one from another and therefore, as they operate, are likely to impede each other. Making policy by the process of elite accommodation between interest groups and government favours incremental policy making through continuous inter-action between the interest group leaders and the policy makers of a single government, be it federal or provincial. The relationship, therefore, is biased in favour of reaching mutually acceptable policy compromises between the government leaders and the interest group representatives con-cerned. Since the major interest groups involved in this process are from the business community, it is obvious that this process favours the interests of business. Also, since it is an ongoing process dealing with problems in an ad hoc way, the system is oriented against long-term planning in favour of case-by-case incrementalism. A major exception occurs when the government perceives a program that it wants and has the bulk of public opinion with it, but this is a rare occurrence (e.g., the National Energy Program). The major concern is likely to be to foster the economic viability of a given business or industry, not necessarily on the basis of economic efficiency but rather of financial viability through government support in one form or another.

This process involves the making of policy in the congenial environ-ment in which like-minded people who are from similar advantaged social backgrounds, with a basis of common social philosophies and class atti-tudes, improvise adaptations to existing policy programs or formulate new ones. The decisions are taken behind closed doors, and representatives of the broad masses of the population are not involved. Generally speak-ing, business interests oppose intervention by government in their opera-tions, and they favour support for business activities through macroeconomic policies. Also, they tend to support policies involving tax incentives, tax expenditures, and so forth, which permit them to retain a larger proportion of the profits from their operations. Generally, they favour the lowering of the burden of taxation that falls on business and ask that government meet the costs of infrastructure support for some of their operations. Also, some business representatives ask for direct government support, such as subsidies or services, or broader support for sectors of the economy encountering severe problems.

The federal dynamic, which involves policy making through interac-tion by the two levels of government, or between two or more provinces, has a different thrust. Here the locus of policy making is in the federal-provincial conference and in the other less formal conferences between governments, federal and provincial. In addition, there are less formal meetings at different bureaucratic levels between governments dealing with specific questions; these will normally be handled by the line departments and can be either bilateral or multilateral. In such encounters, there is a bias in favour of collaborating through programs that are favoured by governments and, therefore, may or may not be acceptable to business and other interests. Major considerations therefore are likely to be the reaching of settlements that respect the legal and constitutional authority of each of the participating governments, and which involve policy decisions that can be readily defended in their respective legislative assemblies and before the mass media. Therefore, it is likely that priority will be given to considerations of equity between provinces and regions over considerations of efficiency and economic viability. There will be many cases where agreement cannot be reached and, therefore, where no solution or settlement occurs. Each side stands on its "principles" and therefore does not "sell out." This leads to complex negotiations and often the striking of postures. Instead of elite accommodation, we have much more of a zero sum process. Often considerations of pride and the need to defend the integrity of one's jurisdiction prevent participants from reaching compromise solutions. Here it is legal distinctions that are at issue where policy accommodation is being sought. While negotiations may at times be in secret, the final result will be in public, where it must be defended. The ultimate responsibility on both sides is that of the elected politicians, concerned about re-election. Here the policy-making community is largely confined to the politicians and their subordinate public officials.

Also the issues that dominate federal-provincial relations at a given time are usually the same ones that concern the interest groups. In short, they are the issues of the day. The recent experience with pricing and regulating the production of petroleum products is a prime example. The modernization of the pulp and paper industry is another. Of course, the concerns of interest groups run far beyond these issues, as every significant industry has its representatives defending its interests in continuous liaison with government people.

This study will explore the two dynamics, the interest group or pluralist one, and the intergovernmental or federal one, with a view to discerning their actual character and experience. The nature of the tension that exists must be probed as it relates to the making of actual, concrete policy. Any further institutionalization or other strengthening of one dynamic could well upset the balance, and frustrate the other; for example, facilitating of the federal-provincial axis could strengthen government in relation to the interest group nexus.

The Problem of Integration

Our examination of the working of these two dynamics, in addition to explaining the mechanisms concerned, will reveal shortcomings and, therefore, point to possible institutional or structural changes. The institutional structures currently in place tend to favour the intergovernmental or federal dynamic, as institutions are elaborated to facilitate this process. On the other hand, the government–interest group relationship is a more unstructured one, which is carried on in the shades of informal contact between government and interest group leaders. Therefore, tensions are less discernible than they would otherwise be.

On the other hand, the elaborate and growing intergovernmental relations structure, which emphasizes constitutional jurisdictions of power and authority, may very well not correspond to any felt need within the community as a whole. Submissions to this Royal Commission seem to de-emphasize the importance of province or region and are much more concerned about the pan-Canadian economy. Does this suggest that the emphasis placed on questions of jurisdiction and power in the hands of different levels of government represents a preoccupation of the politicians, but not of the business leaders and the country at large?

Research has shown that some interest groups are identified with one level of government and others with the other (e.g., federally regulated industries with the federal government, provincially regulated ones with the provincial governments; resource industries with the provincial governments, pan-Canadian transportation and communications industries with the federal government). Is this substantially the case? And if so, what does it signify for policy making? An examination of submissions to the Commission will help clarify these questions.

A thorough ventilation of these alignments and their significance should point to institutional changes and developments in practice which might improve the policy-making process in both the interest group and federal dimensions. Means must be found to meet the complaint of the groups that they are shut out of intergovernmental negotiations, as well as to meet the other complaint that elite accommodation constitutes a privileged form of policy making which is biased in favour of the more advantaged and powerful elements in the population. Business interests complain about internal barriers, costs, delays, and so forth as they try to participate in policy making, especially where two levels of government are involved. Are these claims justified, and if so, how might they be satisfied?

Therefore, there is a need for a systematic examination of the problems and complaints relating to these two processes of policy making, to raise the questions that must be faced as we examine the data and draw our conclusions. A particular focus is the state of the Canadian economic union. Have governments in Canada erected too many non-tariff and other barriers between provinces? And, if so, how might possible institutional and procedural innovations ameliorate the condition?

Chapter 2

The Evolution of Interests in the Canadian Federal System

This chapter deals with the development of economic interests which, over time, matured into the complex economic and industrial structure of present-day Canada. Over the years, the austere and in some ways hostile Canadian environment has developed a close government involvement with private interests, to induce them to undertake to develop the resources and industrial potential of the country. This chapter examines this development through the literature, of which there are two major strands. One is the economic history of Canada, which follows in the pioneering footsteps of Harold Innis, W.A. Mackintosh, Vernon Fowke, George Britnell, W.T. Easterbrook, H.G.J. Aitken and others who developed the particular aspects of the story. The other part of the literature is of more recent origin, although it traces its development from the former strand. This has preserved the name political economy, although it has shifted away from economics to political science and has been influenced by the Marxist critique.

As Innis has shown, Canadian economic history can be explained in terms of the development of staple products for export. The colonial period witnessed a succession of these development processes: the cod fisheries, based mainly on Newfoundland, which emphasized trade with Great Britain and the West Indies; and the fur trade, which drew European traders inland via the St. Lawrence–Great Lakes drainage basin. It was this early fur trade that established the outlines of the east-west economy, based on Montreal, which was made concrete politically in Confederation. The timber trade also followed the waterways inland and involved transportation of a bulk commodity to tidewater for shipment overseas. After this came the wheat economy of the Prairies, which too was oriented toward export from eastern saltwater ports, mainly to European markets. These successive industries contributed to the development of Canada as a primary goods producing country supplying an overseas market, and they were orchestrated by the Canadian commercial interests located primarily in Montreal and later in Toronto.

In the 1860s the commercial and railway interests, mainly located in Montreal, had developed to the point where they could consider extending their sway beyond what was then the United Province of Canada. They conceived of the idea of uniting with the Maritime provinces and later of developing the Prairies. Such a grandiose scheme would require the close collaboration and support of government, and the development of the united transcontinental political union of British North America to carry it forward in the face of rapidly expanding American power. Confederation for Canada, therefore, was a kind of partnership between the major business interests and the governments of the new Dominion, both federal and provincial. From the beginning, both business and government were involved in the cooperative enterprise of economic development. The governments would help finance the railways, which would be the instrument for the development of the transcontinental economy, given the state of technology in the nineteenth century. The development strategy was spelled out in the National Policy contained in the budget of 1879. The federal government would support the construction of the Pacific railway, providing a transcontinental transportation network, and it would also use a system of protective tariffs in order to foster the growth of a Canadian secondary manufacturing industry in partnership with the resource industries, which were geared to export. The east-west export trade in staple products would support the railways. The tariff would support industry, which would find its market in the expanding Canadian frontier, and all of this would be managed by the commercial, banking and railway interests centred in Montreal and Toronto. Since under the Constitution the federal government was assigned most of the powers relating to economic development, there was a kind of partnership between these developmental economic interests and the federal government from the time of Confederation. The provinces, on the other hand, were assigned the cultural, local and private concerns which would permit the French-Canadian elite in the province of Quebec to continue to control educational and social matters.

As it turned out, of course, the provinces in time came to assume a very important role in economic affairs, through control of the public lands (natural resources) and as a result of judicial interpretation of the Constitution, which tended to favour provincial over federal authority. The development of the positive state with its extensive system of social welfare legislation also enhanced the importance and, therefore, the power of the provinces.

Another factor significant in the process was the way in which the staple industries developed after the First World War. This was the time when the minerals of the Canadian Shield and the pulp and paper industry were both developed to serve American markets. The old east-west orientation of the Canadian economy was challenged by a north-south connection, which brought the separate regions of Canada into economic relations with the neighbouring states of the United States. The change inevitably had the effect of enhancing the powers of the provincial governments in relation to the federal, since it was provincial resources that were being exploited, and it downgraded the dominance of the transcontinental railway system, which had been the backbone of Canada. These new economic developments, while enhancing the power and role of the provincial governments, tied them to markets and corporate headquarters located in the United States. This relationship was further enhanced by the development of a secondary manufacturing industry in Central Canada, consisting of subsidiaries of American producers of consumer durables. The effect of these developments was a new tension introduced into the federal system as economic interests came to ally themselves with one or other level of government in their attempts to maximize their own returns. This tension was exacerbated by the resulting uneven economic development, a tendency that has been accentuated with the development of the oil and natural gas industries, the uranium industry and the potash industry. Alliances developed between some provincial governments and industries located within those provinces, challenging the older alliance between the federal government and the railways and the commercial interests associated with them.

A tension also developed between the Central Canadian industrial heartland and the resource industries located on the periphery, going back to the period following the completion of the Canadian Pacific Railway. Prairie farmers felt themselves exploited by a high-cost structure on the railways and by the grain and elevator companies. These they saw in alliance with the banks to whom the farmers owed money which they had borrowed to purchase land and equipment. Therefore, what was expected to be a complementary economic development turned out to be one of complex rivalries and competing interests.

As the Canadian economy has matured in the twentieth century, the north-south connections between Canadian industries and their American affiliates have become more important than the older east-west associations. This has served to increase the power and role of the provincial governments, especially those with rich resource endowments or substantial investments from American corporations. Such investment has come to be sought after by provincial governments anxious to develop local resources and to foster industrialization, and this, in turn, has created an interprovincial rivalry that has sometimes led to provincial protectionist measures. Some industries have developed close associations with their American head offices, which contribute to the economic integration of Canada with the United States. Since many of these industries are closely associated with provincial governments, the result is the implementation of provincial economic development policies that very often conflict with federal ones. The reliance upon the American market as an outlet for Canadian goods has increased, so that now three-quarters of Canadian products sold abroad go to the United States. This situation has intensified as a result of such integrative trade agreements as the Auto Pact and the defence production-sharing arrangements with the United States (Levitt, 1970; Stevenson, 1982; Panitch, 1977; Clement, 1983).

The staple theory of development, first elaborated by H.A. Innis and the other authors cited, was reinterpreted by a new generation of scholars in the 1960s and 1970s. These new political economy scholars had a different concern from their predecessors and followed a newer paradigm. Often informed by the Marxist critique, they discerned patterns of exploitation in the process of economic development. The leading members of this school include Tom Naylor, Garth Stevenson, Jorge Niosi, Larry Pratt, James Richards, H.V. Nelles and Wallace Clement.

Some members of this generation of scholars have identified links between particular interests and one or other level of government. As the groups seek their advantage, sometimes their activities contribute to the decentralization of Canada; and regional capital and foreign-controlled capital sometimes move to support the provincial governments in confrontation with the federal government, or (at times) vice versa. Since natural resources are vested in the Crown in right of the provinces, the driving force in this area tends to be provincial, and regionally based business interests in collaboration with provincial governments can develop alliances that may adversely affect pan-Canadian interests. This virtually inevitable tension between regional and pan-Canadian thrusts in economic development has inspired a rich and often controversial literature, which is examined below.

Provincial dominance in the industrial sector in Ontario sprang from the development of hydro-electric power. Later, other provinces followed Ontario's strategy of development. Given the less sophisticated state of their manufacturing base, they relied upon resource-oriented economic growth. Hydro-electric power became the activating engine for Saskatchewan, Manitoba, New Brunswick and, later, Quebec, British Columbia, and finally Newfoundland (Stevenson, 1982, p. 109). Electricity contributed to the forging of stronger ties between the provinces and the United States because of increased dependence on the New York bond market for financing and, later, on the American market to sell the surplus. To have hydro-electric projects financed at low cost, credit ratings were paramount in the minds of provincial governments, a prevailing concern which helped shape their favourable response to foreign investment and ownership.

The growing dependence upon the United States was acute in the 1960s as provincial and local governments encouraged direct U.S. investment and diverted taxpayers' money into supporting investment by foreign firms (ibid., p. 112), in resources such as uranium in the Algoma district of Ontario, nickel in northern Manitoba, oil in Alberta and Saskatchewan, and iron ore in northern Quebec and Labrador.

Interprovincial competition to attract industrial investment often leads to discriminatory practices, which work at cross-purposes with federal policy. Hydro-Quebec's local preference policy, the Manitoba government's announcement in 1980 that provincial firms would be favoured as suppliers for resource projects, and the Ontario decision in 1977 to opt for a foreign-controlled local firm despite its higher bid over Montreal-based Bombardier to supply rolling stock for the Toronto subway, are examples of provincial protectionism (ibid., pp. 119–24). Moreover, by means of numerous regulations that discourage people from moving elsewhere," The provincial state and its agencies attempt to create attitudes of identification with the province, and thus to attach people more firmly to it (p. 123)." These policies increase citizens' dependence on their provincial governments and foster parochial sentiments (p. 124).

In order to comprehend better the regional nature of the development of the Canadian economic interests, we now examine developments in individual regions.

Ontario

While it is true that Ontario is the province most committed to the pan-Canadian national economy, it is also the province that was the first to claim its own economic autonomy (Armstrong, 1981, pp. 3–5). As early as the turn of the century, the provincial government proceeded to design development programs for the province in areas where nationally elaborated ones failed to promote Ontario's growth. Premier Oliver Mowat, propounding the "Compact theory of Confederation," which argued that Confederation was a kind of treaty between the individual provinces, justified the expansion of Ontario's economic power in the face of the federal authority. The result was several federal-provincial clashes. In this process Ontario was normally defending the interests of corporations that were active within the province.

H.V. Nelles (1973) in his book *The Politics of Development* points out how the Ontario government consistently defended the interests of business, especially in the case of the forest and mining industries. The forest industries, for example, succeeded in inducing the Ontario government to enact legislation to compel the processing of timber cut on Crown lands within the province (Armstrong, 1981, pp. 36–37). This policy was expected to encourage the industrialization of Ontario although it did bring the province into conflict with the federal government, which was at that time favouring trade liberalization.

The Ontario government amended the *Mines Act* in 1900 to force processing within the province. However, this time the private interest was able to gain the support of the federal government, and the province retreated. As Armstrong commented:

> The role of the state in capitalist society includes the provision of assistance to private interests. When jurisdiction is divided by federalism, both levels of government may be looked to for certain kinds of assistance. These interests do not consider the abstract virtues of centralized administration versus local control, but concern themselves with which level is able and willing to provide what they seek. (p. 53)

In short, the business interests fostered their own economic advantage as they sought to involve most levels of government. The federal government was even induced to exercise its power to disallow provincial legislation.

The issue of hydro-electric power constitutes the best example of the use of provincial authority in the support of business. Pressed by industry for cheap power, the Ontario government decided to take over the development of hydro-electric power in order to give its industry an advantage over others. The question of control over the power-producing corporations was referred to the Supreme Court of Canada in 1912, when the provincial government had its claim to jurisdiction sustained. The government of Ontario then created the Ontario Hydro-Electric Power Commission in order to make cheap power available to Ontario industries. When it decided to extend the development of the Ottawa and St. Lawrence Rivers, it found itself embroiled in jurisdictional squabbles with the federal government. Ontario consistently defended the business interests within the province, and this often meant pressing for the extension of the province's powers. As H.V. Nelles observes:

> The Ontario experience seems to indicate that responsibility for vast industrial enterprises narrowed the vision of government and deadened its sense of responsibility to other social groups. Businessmen had succeeded in generalizing their ideology, or in identifying their interests completely with the public interest, largely through their political influence.   (Nelles, 1973, p. 428)

Ontario, therefore was the major champion of provincial rights in the period before the Second World War. This provincialist position is squared by C. Armstrong with Ontario's commitment to Canada:

> The people of Ontario . . . have always considered themselves to be 'real' Canadians and assumed that their wishes are the wishes of the national collectivity. Any apparent conflict between national and provincial objectives may be dissolved by the conviction that the interests of Ontario are the interests of Canada.   (Armstrong, 1981, p. 238)

The example of the government of Ontario was later emulated by other provincial governments. They, too, began to adopt the interests of the businesses located within their boundaries and defended them with whatever means at their disposal in order to further their own economic development. This, of course, produced clashes with business interests in other parts of the country and involved federal-provincial tensions, as each side in a dispute would seek to invoke the powers of whatever level of government seemed to be available. Federal-provincial tension, therefore, naturally increased. As Jorge Niosi commented:

> The federal-provincial conflict does not pit the Canadian bourgeoisie against the multinationals . . . rather it is a question of the emerging bourgeoisie being pitted against the indigenous bourgeoisie, which is becoming increasingly concentrated in Ontario. (Niosi, 1981, p. 34)

Provincial dominance in the industrial sector in Ontario sprang from the development of hydro-electric power, whereas the railways facilitated federal government power. The provincial government then was closely involved with both resource development on the periphery, and industry in the Golden Horseshoe. The postwar years saw the development of an expanded civil service to support economic development through marketing of products and programs to attract investment. Ontario was home to most of the branch plants of U.S. firms, and its officials have worked with them, recently urging them to seek world product mandates now that the conventional branch plant is becoming obsolete as tariffs come down and Canadian production costs outpace American ones. The provincial government has been the champion of its manufacturing sector, fighting to keep power costs low. This meant, for a time, confronting the Conservative government of Alberta on the pricing of petroleum products. However, apart from Ontario Hydro, the government has avoided significant invasion of the preserve of private business (except for the isolated purchase of Suncor shares in 1983). Economic activity has remained in the private sector.

Quebec

The province of Quebec experienced a substantial industrialization around the turn of the century, which was carried out for the most part by English-Canadian and American capital. Through it, the pattern became established that the French-Canadian population supplied the labour force, but management remained in the hands of English-speaking people. After the Second World War the situation came to be resented in French Canada, and after the the death of Premier Maurice Duplessis, the Liberal Party led a reformist surge, which captured the government and ushered in what has come to be known as the Quiet Revolution. Jean Lesage, the new premier, undertook vigorous programs to make Quebeckers "maîtres chez nous." Various public institutions were put in place to facilitate the economic development of the province with substantial government leadership and support. Naturally this was accompanied by substantial "provincial nationalism," which saw the demand for the use of French at the workplace and the development of a French-Canadian managerial and technical structure. In Niosi's words: "The Quiet Revolution established a network of public institutions that have contributed to the development of a francophone bourgeoisie" (ibid., p. 45).

The state created such financial institutions as the Caisse de dépôt et de placement and the Société générale de financement and, through them, has been pumping capital into francophone Quebec businesses.

The result has been the rapid development of a French-speaking managerial elite and of corporations controlled by this elite. The Caisse de dépôt et de placement was given the task of managing the Quebec pension fund and its medicare plan, as well as the investment portfolios of many public and semipublic agencies (ibid.). This powerful thrust by the Lesage government led to some conflict with the federal government, which had longstanding relationships with the major economic interests of Quebec, that were in place before these newer ones were set up. Growing French-Canadian nationalism led to the election of the Parti Québécois in 1976. It was concerned with advancing the cause of French-speaking Quebeckers in both management and the work force generally.

The Quebec economy contains important industrial enterprises which are branches of multinational corporations and which tie that economy to the overall North American one. Quebec industries, therefore, have had to make their peace with this powerful influence. The French-speaking enterprises developed a relationship to the French-speaking state, which supports and, in a sense, protects them. There is therefore, an alliance between the Quebec state and this capitalist interest. In the words of Dorval Brunelle ". . . le projet de souveraineté du Parti québécois peut être considéré comme un projet politique visant à affirmer et à renforcer la bourgeoisie québécoise en se servant de l'État provincial devenue souverain pour assumer sa cohérence" (Brunelle, 1981, p. 160). This position is supported by Anne Legaré, who says that the action of the Parti Québécois is motivated by the desire to rearrange the power relations within the Canadian federation to the advantage of the Québécois francophone interests, particularly those of the petite bourgeoisie (Legaré, 1978, p. 218). The PQ objective, therefore, as seen by these authors, is the growth of Quebec capital in partnership with the state.

The Quebec state proceeded to complete the nationalization of hydroelectricity in 1962 and to develop a state-controlled steel industry (Sidbec). At the same time it enlarged the provincial public service and gave considerable opportunities to young French-Canadian university graduates. The government-established financial institutions have played a major role in the support of Québécois enterprises, such as Provigo, Power Corporation, or Banque d'épargne de Montréal (Fournier, 1978, p. 70).

The provincial government also assisted cooperatives, supported the growth of state corporations and launched financial and technical aid programs for small- and medium-sized enterprises (ibid., p. 71). Pierre Fournier comments that the PQ has not sought to confront American capital, but rather to substitute itself for the Canadian bourgeoisie, claiming a better place for Quebec interests under the general sway of American multinationals (ibid., p. 76). This saw an alliance between the Quebec government and the credit unions (caisses populaires) to resist the Canadian banks and the federal government. Niosi does not go as far as Fournier: "All francophone capitalists, it would seem, seek the support of the Quebec government to some degree. It is in their collective interest to strengthen the Quebec government but not to the extent of separating from the rest of Canada. . . . the larger a corporation is, the less it wants to be identified with an ethnic group" (Niosi, 1981, p. 63). On the other hand, the Quebec government appears to be tightening its control over the public corporations (Fournier, 1983, p. 210). Among the effected changes figure: government-appointed management and members of the board; and a greater say by government in determining budgets, as well as increased authority over projects undertaken by the corporations. The PQ has tended to appoint its own civil servants to the boards of these corporations as a means of maintaining contact and influence. Another tie between the Quebec government and French-Canadian capital comes through the purchase of Quebec bonds by the caisses populaires. In times of crisis, the willingness to buy these securities is often a crucial matter in helping the government of Quebec over difficult conditions.

The Société générale de financement is another example of a state corporation bridging the gap between government and francophone capital. Its first mandate was to rescue threatened family-run companies with emergency funds. Later it became a state corporation (1973). Its task was to establish Quebec industrial complexes and to participate in the management and financing of medium-sized and large Quebec firms. It has served to facilitate the mergers and other cooperative arrangements between small- and medium-sized firms with growth potential in order to make them more competitive (ibid., p. 216).

However, the most important instrument of the Quebec government in dealing with industry is Hydro-Quebec. The government was successful in gaining the financial support of a consortium of American banks in order to raise the capital to purchase the private power companies and complete Hydro-Quebec in the first place. Once created, it became an instrument supplying power for the private sector in Quebec and, therefore, became an important influence over it. In turn Hydro-Quebec is so organized that the Quebec government has substantial power over its policies.

Now protected by this array of new state institutions and state-supported institutions, and supported by promotional bodies such as the Société québécoise d'initiative agro-alimentaire (Soquia) and the Société québécoise d'exploration minière (Soquem) (and also the producing bodies, such as the steel industry Sidbec), the hand of government extends in many ways to assist the development of Quebec-based, francophone capital. The Banque Nationale, after enlarging its branch network by absorbing other banking institutions, now has over 50 percent of the Canadian chartered bank branches in the province of Quebec. In addition, the Mouvement Desjardins has been entrusted with a substantial portion of the savings of Quebecers. Therefore, there is now in place a substantial French-speaking Québécois institutional structure and concentration of capital capable of supporting a substantial number of small- and medium-sized companies. A viable and fairly autonomous French-speaking bourgeoisie may now be said to exist which, naturally, is expected to support the government of Quebec in its relations with the federal government.

This loyalty was put to the test in 1982, when the Caisse de dépôt et placement du Québec indicated an interest in increasing its holdings of shares of Canadian Pacific Limited from the 9.4 percent then held. The management of Canadian Pacific became alarmed, as did the federal government, which introduced Bill S–31 in the Senate to prohibit provincial government bodies from owning more than 10 percent of voting shares in designated businesses under federal jurisdiction, or any voting shares acquired after November 2, 1982. The bill was intended to apply to the transportation sector because of its "uniquely national" character, and thereby to enable the federal government to protect its own jurisdiction from possible attempts by provincial governments to discriminate against other provinces or evade federal regulatory authority.

The bill was strongly attacked by the Quebec government, of course. The Canadian Chamber of Commerce and Canadian Pacific supported the federal government. However, the francophone business leaders in Quebec strongly supported the Caisse, led by Pierre Lortie, president of the Montreal Stock Exchange, arguing that francophone business was seriously underrepresented in the Canadian corporate world and that Quebec government agencies should, indeed act to correct this wrong. Also, they favoured an interventionist role for government in economic affairs (Tupper, 1983; Pollard, 1984, pp. 71–73).

Atlantic Canada

In a sense the development of the Atlantic provinces is a kind of obverse of that of the provinces of Ontario and the West. These two richer regions, because of their capacity to attract capital and build up an industrial structure, and also because of their rich resource base, were able to undertake aggressive policies of "province-building." The Atlantic provinces, on the other hand, are the poorest-endowed of all of the regions of Canada and, therefore, share more with Quebec than with the richer provinces west of the Ottawa River. However, unlike Quebec, the Atlantic provinces are all small, with weak economic bases. Also they are anglophone (except for the small Acadian population) and, therefore, do not have the distinctive will to preserve their language, which is so characteristic of Quebec.

At the time of Confederation, Nova Scotia was probably, on a per capita basis, the wealthiest province of Canada. At least it was one that had experienced a rich economic development based upon commerce, carried out throughout the world in wooden sailing vessels. As a result, there was a vigorous spirit of enterprise and independence. New Brunswick, too, had been a prosperous province with its rich stands of pine, which became the major source of masts for the Royal Navy. However, these provinces entered Confederation looking to find in the union with Canada a solution to a crisis that technology brought to them. The steam engine was the agent for undermining the Maritime economy. Inserted into steel-hulled vessels it became the new means of sea transportation which eclipsed the wooden sailing ships that were the basis for the Maritime economy. Put on wheels it became the basis for the railways that made possible the vision of Canada from Atlantic to Pacific. However, this very vision carried within it the seeds of Central Canadian industrial expansion, partly at the cost of the smaller and peripherally situated industries of the Maritime provinces.

The Maritimes, therefore, were compelled to seek some alternative arrangement for their obsolescent economy, and to do so quickly, because the Americans had abrogated the reciprocity treaty that had provided them with the essential markets for survival. Confederation then was the only recourse for the Maritimes, which were really compelled to enter into association with the rest of British North America, hoping that in the long run this would offer a solution to their economic difficulties.

At first, Maritime business believed that the established industries of the Maritime provinces would be able to compete effectively with what were at that time — in some ways — less developed industries in the United Province of Canada. However, the relatively small population and the isolated location of the Maritime provinces in relation to Central Canada made effective industrial competition impossible. When the Maritimes were linked with Central Canada, the way was open to a flood of industrial products from that area, and the Eastern provinces entered into a long period of economic stagnation and relative decline.

This situation placed the governments of the Maritime provinces in a very different situation from that of the other provinces. Since they were all "have-not" provinces, they came to depend upon the federal government more and more as time went on. This meant they did not have the same bargaining power, or "weight," within the federation as did their larger and wealthier neighbours. In the twentieth century, they naturally tended to side with their benefactor, the federal government, when other provinces began to reach for greater autonomy. This greater dependence of the Maritime provinces on the federal government tended to preserve clientele political relationships that were soon abandoned west of the Ottawa River. The traditional political arrangements persisted, and migration patterns (mainly migration out of the region to the rest of Canada or to the United States) meant that there was very little infusion of new blood via immigration into the Maritime provinces.

Newfoundland, of course, is a special case. It did not enter Confederation until 1949, after it emerged from the Commission of Government arrangement in which it was a virtual ward of the British government from the time of the Depression until its entry into Canada. The province entered as much the poorest province in Canada, although its endowment of natural resources appears to be considerably richer than that of the Maritimes. However, it remains relatively underdeveloped, and in order to attract capital it has been led to make overly generous concessions to whatever capitalist interests were willing to invest and undertake economic activity. The result has been the bitter experience of having to make overly generous concessions to outsiders in order to bring about economic activity. Some of these undertakings have turned out to be economically nonviable. Particularly hard has been the Churchill Falls development in which the province has been held to a long-term contract to sell electric power to Hydro-Quebec at prices that reflect the cheap energy prices of the period before the oil shocks in the early 1970s.

Newfoundland's relations with Ottawa have been much more turbulent than those of the Maritime provinces. The province's experience with outside capital has made it particularly wary and demanding. Friction developed between the federal government and the government of Newfoundland on the question of offshore oil development, with the result that slow progress has been made in developing this potentially rich resource.

The pattern of reliance on the federal government went furthest in the case of the fishing industry. It had long been supported on a piecemeal basis out of the federal treasury to help it modernize and develop packing plants for the catch. However, the aggressive foreign assault on the fishing banks by highly capitalized, modern ships and facilities threatened to bankrupt the Canadian industry. Therefore the federal government, after receiving the report of the Kirby Task Force on the Fishery, proceeded to rationalize the industry by consolidating the private fishing and fish-packing companies and setting up, with both federal and provincial government support and that of a major chartered bank, one consolidated industry, Fish Products International. It is not yet apparent whether this rescue operation will produce a viable industry. (Currently the trawler men are on strike, and the inshore fishermen are still earning very low incomes.)

Taken as a whole, the Atlantic provinces, in their relationship with the federal government and with the other provinces, have been in a weak bargaining position. They have attracted considerable regional development assistance from the federal government and have also been able to borrow money from Alberta. Despite these infusions of outside capital, the general well-being of the population still trails that of the rest of Canada, if one considers rates of employment and average wages and salaries. On the other hand, there is a considerable loyalty on the part of the population to the region, and considerable pride in a way of life that has preserved much gentility and a human scale of activity which is highly prized.

The New West

As we have seen, the Prairie provinces were the home of the wheat economy, which was developed around the turn of the century as part of the economic development program outlined in the National Policy of 1879. Based on the railway and European export markets for Canadian grain, the three Prairie provinces were a major component of the east-west economy. However, just as that economic system was turned around in the 1920s in Ontario with the development of the pulp and paper and base metals industries, so in Western Canada it was undermined by the development of the new resource industries, particularly petroleum, natural gas, uranium and potash.

The Western population, which had come to resent the dominance of outside interests, especially as manifested through the grain companies, the railways and the banks, found a means of expressing its discontent when the opportunities arose to re-orient their economies on the basis of new resource industries.

Indeed, the provincial government reaction in Alberta, emphasizing business-government cooperation, parallels very closely the attitudes of the government of Ontario (Pratt, 1977, p. 133). The key was a rising, ambitious class of indigenous business entrepreneurs, urban professionals and state administrators who perceived an opportunity for the development of the provincial economy through the partnership of business and government. Through this means, the province's reliance on external economic and political forces could be drastically reduced, and its economy diversified to be self-sustaining before the oil and natural gas reserves were depleted. To accomplish this goal, reliance was placed upon provincial powers as the shield against possible federal inroads, that were anticipated to claim, for the nation as a whole, overly large shares of the resource rents. Naturally, this led to a new regional consciousness in Western Canada, which in turn supported the creation of various joint ventures between the private and public sectors that came to symbolize the new "people's capitalism" (Pratt and Richards, 1979, p. 242).

The process set in motion a new determination to supersede Central Canada and its establishment, even if this meant confronting the federal government. The emphasis was, therefore, on an aggressive acquisition of resource rents, and so Alberta's relationship with the oil and gas industry was not always harmonious. While the province and the industry made common cause on those issues concerned to prevent undue federal encroachment, they found themselves rivals for the rents of these resources.

The threat to withdraw capital and move drilling rigs out of the province was always a consideration for the provincial government, which prevented it from increasing its taxation beyond a certain point. Pratt and Richards comment that "the comfortable assumption that the interest of the major oil companies and Alberta's interests are identical is now questioned on both sides, and this divergence of outlook could well increase as competition for scarce resources intensifies" (Pratt, 1977, p. 155). A role for the government developed to encourage the growth of local capital. For example, it purchased Pacific Western Airlines (PWA) in 1974 to help diversify the provincial economy. "The airline has been placed under the control of some of the government's closest business allies" (ibid.). Similarly, the Alberta Energy Company, partly owned by the government and partly by private capital, is playing a role in the Syncrude oil sands project. This arrangement offers a means for the government to undertake joint ventures, and it also serves to advance the careers of many young Alberta professionals. In short, this state entrepreneurial spirit reflected a provincial economic 'nationalism' that was strongly supported by a rising middle class.

Positive government in the outlying areas was implemented to foster industrial growth, decentralization and the consolidation of the regional bourgeoisie. The goals that Ontario had pursued during the formative years of its industrial development constituted the credo of the ruling Conservative party in the Alberta of 1971: "The synthesis of business and politics" (ibid., p. 133). The role of the state in planning and promoting the province's economic development was perceived by an ambitious rising class of "indigenous business entrepreneurs, urban professionals, and state administrators" (ibid.) as essential for its advancement. At the outset of the 1970s, a growing labour force was swelling the ranks of the service sector, so the new middle class was composed of managerial, professional and white-collar workers. The main purposes of this new class was to tighten its hold on the Alberta economy, to diminish the province's reliance on external economic and political forces, and to diversify the province's economy before the depletion of the oil and natural gas reserves (ibid.)

Local Alberta entrepreneurial efforts were led by an *arriviste bourgeoisie* (Pratt and Richards, 1979, p. 167), whose aim was to weld the private and public sectors into a coherent unit. It was inspired and directed by a handful of owners and managers of a few Alberta-based corporations with the required resources to compete at the national and international levels. Upwardly mobile professionals such as "corporate lawyers, economic and financial assistants, engineers, geologists, and other scientists or technical experts . . ." (ibid.) as well as the state-administrative elite — in short, the custodians of Alberta's wealth and interest — took up the tasks of funnelling financial surpluses into profitable ventures and mapping out strategies for the province's future prosperity (ibid.).

Dedicated to local industrial growth, this elite viewed the province as the most accessible political sphere for the promotion of its interest. Provincial powers could protect it from federal inroads into Alberta's resource base — its jealously guarded jurisdictional precinct.

There is a certain similarity in the way in which the governments of Alberta and Quebec express their desire for autonomy and economic independence. Both are apprehensive of control from outside the province, and both are concerned about possible actions by the federal government. Therefore, they are prepared to take defensive action against external encroachments on provincial jurisdiction over resource ownership and control. As Pratt and Richards comment, "Western business supports constitutional decentralization and a strong, positive state at the provincial level as a buffer against a predatory national government" (ibid., p. 234). The keystone of diversification is the world-scale petrochemical complex that the Alberta government has undertaken to build. This, however, is likely to encounter competition from Petrosar, located in Sarnia, Ontario, which is closer to markets. Committed to capitalism, as the Alberta government is, it encounters the uneven distribution of investment that a free-market economy involves. In Alberta's case, there is relatively little investment in secondary processing from outside the province.

Saskatchewan, ruled by a New Democratic Party government in the 1970s, was less successful than its neighbour in building up an autonomous, capitalist entrepreneurial group. Instead, the government relied upon Crown corporations. The business community of the province, however, had its reservations about such a policy. Moreover, the private interests in the potash industry, supported by the federal government, took the Saskatchewan government to court when it attempted to prorate the production of potash and to impose a royalty structure. After such difficulties, the government finally determined on a policy of nationalization of part of the potash industry. Then there would be no question of potentially unconstitutional taxation, and the government could argue that it had no option but nationalization in view of the legal obstacles lying in the way of taxation and royalty policies.

British Columbia, with its wealth concentrated in forestry and mining (86 percent of the province's exports), which it sends to the United States and now Japan, has taken a very protective attitude toward these industries. It has prevented the sale of MacMillan Bloedel to Canadian Pacific Investments, while raising no objection to growing U.S. and Japanese holdings. The provincial government's main concern has been to encourage industrial diversification from the forest-industry base and to improve the management of the forest to achieve steady sustained yields. The mining industry has been an important but volatile component in the province's economy, one demanding amounts of investment capital that have strained the province's capabilities. The province's isolation beyond the Rocky Mountains and its preoccupation with its distinctive problems have produced feelings of distance from eastern Canada and the federal power.

Two Dynamics

In short, since the challenge to the east-west economy after the turn of the century, there have been two dynamics at work in Canada: one toward centralization and the other toward decentralization. Some elements of the business community, because of the nature of their industries and their location, find their interests closer to one level of government, while others find theirs closer to the other. And some side on one issue with the federal government, and on other issues with the provinces. The diffusion of power inherent in federalism naturally left areas of uncertainty which private interests could exploit. With the courts' narrow construction of the federal power over trade and commerce in the early part of the century, the provinces, led by Ontario, were able to lay claim to more powers than hitherto. As Nelles comments, "Paternal government departments and political friendships permitted businessmen to use the state to stabilize, extend and legitimize their economic power" (Nelles, 1973, p. 427). Provincial politicians and public servants naturally were willing to go along with the expansion of their own power and authority.

The business community did not approach these jurisdictional questions from a dogmatic stance. Its concern was to maximize its own freedom and advantage. In Armstrong's words, "The only things that capital consistently supports are its own interests, and when these have been threatened by aggressive provincial governments, businesses unhesitatingly pushed for a stronger central government. . . . About all that can be concluded is that big business understands that a federal system provides interest groups with a number of potential sources of leverage and veto points, and that capital . . . has no permanent allies or enemies, only permanent interests" (Armstrong, 1981, pp. 233–34).

In Quebec where predominant power was in the hands of anglophone corporations headquartered outside the province, one finds a tendency toward state-managed development, as the government collaborated with indigenous francophone business interests. This was greatly intensified after 1976 with the election of the Parti Québécois.

In the case of both Quebec and the West, there is a similar desire on the part of local capitalist interests to resist external control, and this includes control from the federal government. This led very conservative business interests to put aside their reservations about state activity in the economy and to collaborate with the provincial government in order to build up an autonomous provincial capital base. As the political economy authors (Stevenson, Levitt, Clement) argue, uneven development in Canada has created economic enclaves on the periphery and has often led them to make common cause with foreign capital. However, these are not permanent commitments and a good number of such interests are cooperating with federal and also with provincial authority. If one is to make sense of the pull-haul of interests in Canada, one must first be aware of the regional economic interests and their interaction with those of a more pan-Canadian orientation.

Chapter 3

The Recent Development of Canadian Federalism

The century and more of Canadian federal association has witnessed a changing relationship between the federal and provincial governments within the largely unchanging framework of the country's constitutional arrangements. (Perhaps the Charter of Rights and Freedoms will bring significant changes, but that is for the future.) Each level is ultimately forced to find accommodation with the other. Sometimes there have been conflicts, more often there has been more-or-less willing cooperation. No doubt the distribution of powers worked most harmoniously in the earlier period, as one would expect, out of proximity to the period in which the Constitution was framed. Over the years, Maritime discontent, Quebec separatism and Western alienation have never reached the point of ultimate confrontation; in the final analysis a modus vivendi has always been found.

With the development of the positive state in the twentieth century to meet the problems of urbanization and industrialization, the federal and provincial governments were led to cooperate, so that the required services that often lay within provincial jurisdiction could be supplied with federal financial aid. Conditional subsidies or grants-in-aid began in 1913 with the *Agricultural Instruction Act*, followed in 1919 by the *Technical Instruction Act*, by which the provinces supplied the instruction and received federal funds to pay half of the costs. In 1919 the federal government made funds available to assist the provinces in making highway construction possible. Similar programs were instituted to control venereal diseases (1919) and to set up labour exchanges (Maxwell, 1937). With the setting up of old age pensions on a federal-provincial cooperative basis in 1926, the scale and bureaucratic commitment of cooperative programs became substantial.

The coming of the Depression in 1929 soon created conditions that compelled the federal government to come to the aid of hard-pressed provinces. It paid 40 percent of poor relief costs from 1930 to 1937 and lent the Western provinces $106 million. Then the destitution in the West led the federal government to pay all the relief costs of hard-hit provinces. These conditions went far beyond the capacity of the Canadian Constitution to handle; hence, the Royal Commission on Dominion-Provincial Relations (the Rowell-Sirois Commission) was set up to find solutions.

The Commission reported in 1940, making suggestions for cooperative arrangements to overcome the jurisdictional difficulties. In particular, it was concerned with the problem caused by the concentration of wealth in the major cities of Central Canada, which meant that only the provincial governments in which these cities were located could tax these pools of wealth, along with the federal government (which had a general power to tax). It made suggestions for special adjustment grants to be made to the poorer provinces to enable them to carry out their obligations in rendering social services and providing public facilities, such as roads, up to a satisfactory Canadian standard.

Since the Commission reported in the midst of the Second World War, its recommendations were used as a reservoir of suggestions to facilitate adaptation to wartime conditions. The federal government, for the emergency period, took over the essential powers to direct the economy and proceeded to invade provincial areas of taxation, but it compensated the provinces by making grants so that their capacity to render services would not be impaired. Thus, the major thrust of the Royal Commission's recommendations came to be implemented as wartime arrangements. Once the war was over, the federal government succeeded in extending the wartime tax arrangements by negotiating tax rental agreements and, later, tax-sharing arrangements, with the provinces. Following the recommendations in the White Paper on Employment and Income, the federal government took the initiative in Canada's external economic relations by signing the General Agreement on Tariffs and Trade (GATT) and generally participating vigorously in international economic activities.

The provinces made no objection at first to these initiatives because they had neither the bureaucratic competence nor the experience to pursue vigorous economic policies beyond their borders. These were prosperous years, when Canadians were confident of their future and saw their wealth and the demand for their products expanding.

However, some provincial leaders became apprehensive at what they perceived to be a federal government takeover of some traditional provincial powers. The Quebec government, in particular, took the initiative by refusing to sign the tax rental agreements. This forced the federal government to develop a scheme whereby Quebec would not suffer discrimination, even if it did not sign an agreement. There followed a period of accommodation of Quebec's demands, which led other provinces to follow the Quebec lead and ask for similar concessions. The door was open to continued federal-provincial disagreement over the sharing of revenues and the size of transfer payments.

The federal government was carrying out the role prescribed for it by the Rowell-Sirois Commission to tax the pools of wealth in Central Canada and distribute them to areas of need. This arrangement was an acceptable one as long as relations between the two orders of government were good, and as long as the country was prosperous. The federal government assumed the role of the great equalizer, the honest broker between the different regions of Canada.

However, the provinces, and in particular Quebec, were apprehensive about the federal government's assumption of the dominant role in the field of public finance in Canada. Provincial political leaders, especially in provinces that were net contributors or exporters of tax revenues, came to resent the fact that the federal government alone was deciding on the disposition of funds to which they were contributing. Tensions between the two orders grew, even as the numbers of cooperative programs between them increased.

An inventory published by Alberta listed 110 cooperative programs in 1981. While many of these were specific to local installations, others were substantial and important programs relating to such vital matters as the Canada Assistance Plan, the Canada Manpower Industrial Training Program, Established Programs Financing, Fiscal Equalization Payments, or Fiscal Stabilization Payments to Provinces. Together they form a network of government which enables the country to function through the maze of elaborate jurisdictional overlaps that is beyond the scope of this study to analyze.

At the interprovincial level, there have also been cooperative programs. For example, the Council of Ministers of Education of Canada (CMEC) was organized in 1967 to provide a mechanism for consultation among the provincial ministers of education. Annual meetings are held, as well as other regular ones. Individual provinces retain their full jurisdiction over their own policies, but CMEC facilitates the exchange of information and some harmonization of policies. There is a secretariat in Toronto, headed by a full-time executive director with a staff of about twenty-five. The main issues dealt with have included financing arrangements for post-secondary education, the provision of adequate funding for the Bilingualism in Education Program, and the educational use of satellites. The secretariat organizes the numerous meetings for the council and its committees, which include federal-provincial working groups.

These intergovernmental cooperative arrangements take place unobtrusively and harmoniously. Through them many of the obstacles that federalism might have invited are overcome. They are characterized by the kind of working together that is possible among people who are committed to a common objective. Therefore, the success seems to be greater in areas where the line departments are concerned to carry out a given program of action. In the field in which the government leadership (prime minister and cabinet and senior officials) is involved, concern over jurisdictional powers is more likely to lead to rivalry and conflict.

The new rivalry between the federal and provincial governments led each side to build up its administrative and decision-making capacity, especially during the 1960s and 1970s. Even the governments of the poorer provinces, now supported by federal funds, were able to afford this bureaucratic enhancement. Provinces developed the competence to defend their own areas of jurisdiction and to develop sophisticated economic policies. They recruited economists, statisticians and lawyers, who, working with the leading economic interest groups in the province, assisted in formulating the provincial development strategies that we have come to refer to as province-building. This led to vigorous challenges to the federal authority by provincial governments. In the Western provinces in particular, many politicians felt that their new-found wealth was being unfairly tapped by the federal government for distribution to other parts of Canada. They reacted by attempting to build up their own economies, especially processing and manufacturing, under provincial government leadership; and this encouraged the economic balkanization of the country. Some provincial governments used their powers to license economic activity in order to protect local workers from competition from beyond their borders. Gradually, the Canadian common market began to show cracks along provincial boundaries, producing rivalry and competition between regions, and preventing many Canadian industries from achieving economies of scale in an era of mass production.

Differences in per capita income persisted despite ambitious federal programs of equalization and stabilization. Morever, the differences were now well known to the governments and peoples of the deprived provinces, where unemployment was high and incomes were low. So disparities became a sensitive issue.

Following the federal example, provincial governments proceeded to gird themselves with intergovernmental relations departments — teams of experts skilled in federal-provincial diplomacy. The easy cooperation between line departments was now downplayed in favour of a new, more intense adversarial relationship between governments routed increasingly through these quasi-diplomatic channels. These relationships tend to resemble international politics in their zero-sum, rivalry perspectives. As the economic crisis of the 1970s deepened, governments became concerned to protect their revenue sources and to foist obligations for expensive services and other burdens onto the other order of government.

These moves have led the federal government to greater centralization of its activities. The government was reorganized in January 1982. A new and short-lived Ministry of State for Economic and Regional Development (MSERD) was built around the previous Ministry of State for

Economic Development, with the development functions of the Department of Regional Economic Expansion added to it. (Mr. Turner terminated this arrangement.) Parallel to this was the splitting of the Department of Industry, Trade and Commerce, sending the trade commissioner service to the Department of External Affairs. A new Department of Regional Industrial Expansion (DRIE) was created from industrial development parts of the old Department of Trade and Commerce, combined with most of the Department of Regional Economic Expansion and the Ministry of State to Assist Small Business and Tourism. The idea was to make policy pan-Canadian without the regional biases of the previous organizational structure. It was hoped that this would place greater emphasis on developing the efficiency of the overall Canadian economy.

This centralization was strengthened by the creation of the new Federal Economic Development Coordinators (FEDCs). These are senior civil servants sent out to the regions to coordinate federal economic programs and to work out relationships with their provincial opposite members. These senior officials can serve as prefects representing the federal government in the field, as well as increasing federal government sensitivity to conditions in the provinces by having senior officials on site.

Following this reorganization, one can identify eight distinct trends in federal-provincial relations:

1. An increasing use of unilateral action, especially by the federal government, without consultation with the other order of government.
2. An increasing preference by the federal government for direct delivery of programs instead of joint programs.
3. A greater emphasis on visibility and accountability of federal funds transferred to provincial governments.
4. Growing evidence of cutbacks in federal transfer payments to the provincial governments.
5. An effort by the federal government to combat decentralist forces and re-establish "national standards."
6. A prevalent feeling of mistrust and suspicion between the two orders of government, largely as a result of unilateral action, cutbacks and withdrawal from joint programs.
7. An increasing preference by both orders of government for bilateral federal-provincial meetings instead of the first ministers' conferences of the 1970s.
8. A decline in the level of overt federal-provincial conflict, resulting in an "uneasy truce."

Many of these elements overlap and the breakdown into the above categories is somewhat artificial. Some federal initiatives would fit into several categories. In particular, the increasing emphasis on unilateral action, visibility and accountability, direct delivery and national standards, leading to an increase in suspicion and mistrust, are central elements of the "new federalism." These are separate aspects of the federal-provincial relationship; hence, each is examined separately.

Unilateral Action

In 1978, Louis Bernard, a senior Quebec official in the Intergovernmental Affairs Department, cited unilateral action by the federal government as a major factor in the poor relations developing between the federal and provincial governments (Bernard, 1979). Since that time, unilateral action has become even more pronounced. The threat to patriate the Constitution unilaterally and the introduction of the National Energy Program in 1980 are prime examples.

Mr. Trudeau acknowledged that his government took a new direction in dealing with the provincial governments after his return to power in 1980:

> We are going to do what is good for the people, and if you don't like it, take us to the courts or take us to the people. Our view of federalism was being eroded because we were trying to be . . . cooperative during most of the sixties and seventies and thinking that we could build and fortify the national will by never fighting with the provinces.[1]

The prime minister argued that the federal government would be weakened if it were required to secure agreement with the provinces. His logic was: If you tell the premiers that you need agreement, they will withhold it until they get what they want. You get better results if you say you would like agreement; but if you do not get it, you will act in the way you see fit within your powers.

As the Liberal federal government came to view consensus as a luxury that it could not always afford, it began to abandon the effort to achieve it. Consultation with the provinces on issues that clearly affected them, whether or not they were strictly within the jurisdiction of one or other of the governments, at times was neglected.

The federal government unilaterally amended the 1977 *Established Programs Financing Act*, both in 1982 and in 1983, even though there had been no negotiations since 1981. In December 1983, the federal minister of health unveiled a new *Canada Health Act*, which established conditions that the provinces must meet if they are to receive federal funding. Even though health care is entirely within provincial jurisdiction, no consultation took place prior to the drafting of the bill.

In May 1983, the federal government tabled Bill C-155, which provided for major changes to the Western grain transportation system, including the abandonment of the statutory Crow Rate. The federal government was acting within its own jurisdiction, although the impact of this initiative on the prairie economy woud necessarily have implications for the provincial governments. The Saskatchewan government stated in a brief to the House of Commons Standing Committee on Transportation: "As a provincial government we are particularly concerned about any changes to the statutory grain rates because our economy is significantly affected by our agricultural sector.[2] The provincial governments were not part of the consultative process undertaken by the Gilson task force, prior to the drafting of its report. The task force consulted the various groups and individuals in the West and after deciding upon its course of action, the federal government acted unilaterally. Similarly, the Atlantic provinces were concerned when they learned of the federal government's unilateral review of Maritime freight subsidies.

Relating to justice policy, the federal government introduced legislation which provided for the creation of a civilian security intelligence service without prior consultation with the provincial governments, which are constitutionally responsible for the administration of justice.

When talks with the Newfoundland provincial government failed, the federal government announced unilaterally, in July 1983, a plan to restructure the fisheries. (In September, the two governments reached an accord, which prevailed over the July plan.) This was followed a few days later by an announcement that the federal government was re-assuming administrative control over fisheries in Quebec — something that had been devolved to the province in 1922. No consultation preceded this announcement.

Since the Liberals were defeated in September 1984, the Conservatives have indicated a desire to work out compromises with the provinces, so the trend to unilateralism may be reversed. However, this remains to be seen. Governments always assume office seeking good relations. The test comes in the detailed process of intergovernmental and government-group negotiations.

Emphasis on Direct Delivery

Dissatisfaction with the lack of visibility and accountability in shared-cost programs led the federal government to favour the direct delivery of its own programs over joint programming with the provincial governments. In his brief to the Royal Commission on the Economic Union and Development Prospects for Canada, Donald Johnston, the minister of state for economic development, spoke of refining the relationship between the two levels of government in matters of economic development. Acknowledging that they have different responsibilities under the Constitution in this field, he asserted that it was logical for there to be "direct" or "parallel" delivery of programs. Thus, there was a greater tendency for the federal government to fund projects directly, bypassing the provincial governments.

An example of this relates to rural development in Newfoundland. When a five-year joint agreement for rural development funding ended in 1983, the provincial government was anxious for a replacement. The federal government unilaterally decided that there was no need for a joint agreement, especially since it was contributing 90 percent of the cost; it decided to fund the projects directly.

This same philosophy was inherent in the Economic and Regional Development Agreements (ERDAs), which were to replace the ten-year umbrella General Development Agreements (GDAs) that had been signed by the federal government with each of the provinces in 1974. Whereas the GDAs, at least initially, emphasized joint federal-provincial delivery of economic development programs, the emphasis within the ERDAs was on coordinated planning between the two levels of government but parallel delivery of services.

Underlying this approach is the inherent belief that each government can best determine the policies that fall within its jurisdiction. This is closely linked to unilateral action without consultation. This emphasis did not emanate solely from Ottawa. The Quebec government tried to pass legislation in 1983 (Bill 38) which sought to protect the province's exclusive jurisdiction over municipal affairs by penalizing any municipality that accepted funds from the federal government. For its part, the federal government wanted to supervise projects that it was partially funding through the New Employment Expansion and Development program. This separation of its relations with provincial governments from those with interest groups gives the federal government greater flexibility and room to manoeuvre.

Emphasis on Visibility and Accountability of Federal Funds

A key element of the new federalism concerned the federal attitude toward payments transferred to the provinces. Unhappy with the lack of visibility and accountability of its funds under the 1977 Established Programs Financing arrangements, the federal government sought to attain greater control over these payments. Prime Minister Trudeau reaffirmed in 1983 that, "Cooperative federalism is dead . . . in the sense that the federal government is expected to hand money over to the provinces for them to spend in any which way."[3] Ottawa introduced the *Canada Health Act*, which affirmed national standards for provincial health insurance programs and provided for sanctions to be applied to provinces that failed to meet federally determined national standards. Moreover, it required that the provinces supply information to the federal government concerning the operation of their programs.

The federal government felt that it was not getting enough visibility (i.e., credit) for programs to which it was contributing substantial amounts. Mr. Trudeau asserted that "when the federal government was giving taxpayers' money to assist the provinces on some project, it was essential

that the taxpayers realize the use and employment of the funds."[4]
"Appropriate recognition" of federal funding for provincial health insurance programs was required under the terms of the proposed *Canada Health Act.*

Moreover, an amendment was introduced to the 1977 *Established Programs Financing Act* (EPF), suggesting a greater attempt to control funds transferred to the provinces. The EPF arrangements were founded on the principle of "block funding"; i.e., the provinces could divide a federal transfer payment as they saw fit between the health and the post-secondary components, or indeed they could simply spend it as they wished.

Bill C–150, reintroduced in 1984 as C–12, effectively separated Ottawa's contribution to health and post-secondary education, arbitrarily assuming a division between the two components, and then determining the federal contribution by subjecting each component to a different increase cap. This undermines the principle of unseverable block funding.

Cutbacks in Federal Funding

The provincial governments have complained about reductions in the federal financial commitments to provincial programs, especially for health and post-secondary education. An amendment to the 1977 EPF legislation was introduced in the House of Commons on May 2, 1983[5] with no prior consultation with the provinces. This bill established the level of the federal government's cash contribution to the provinces; and subsequently the increase in the education portion was capped to fit the federal government's "6-and-5" restraint program.

There were three consequences. The revenue the provinces would receive for social programming was limited; a retreat from the principle of block funding was signalled; and the element of predictability, which had accompanied the establishment of EPF financing in 1977, was removed. The provinces now live from year to year under the threat of severe financial cutbacks imposed by the federal government. An Alberta government document stated: "These amendments highlight the federal government's determination to proceed unilaterally in an area which has a direct effect on the provinces' fiscal capacity."[6]

Re-establishing National Standards

In a meeting with Western news media representatives in Ottawa on July 8, 1983, Prime Minister Trudeau stated:

> I think there has been an attempt to weaken the right and the duty of the national government to speak for all of Canada, as it must, since it is the only government which, territorially, encompasses all Canada. Executive federalism, therefore, cannot be substituted for what I hold to be a basic principle of federalism: that when the national will can be demonstrated to be

superior over a regional will, the national will must prevail. . . . But what is good, what is in the interests of Canada? To me the Canadian national good is more important than a provincial national good, and therefore there should be a national will expressed by Canadians through their government when such conflicts arise, and they should be settled, if necessary, by election or by referenda and not by sort of a weighing of persons as Executive Federalism.[7]

The attempt to establish and maintain national standards is perhaps most obvious in the proposed Canada Health Act. The new act is designed primarily to ensure that national standards for insured medical and hospital services are clarified and maintained. It includes appropriate sanctions for provinces that refuse to meet the national standards in their provincial programs.

Feelings of Mistrust and Suspicion

Louis Bernard gave a personal reflection on the state of federal-provincial relations in 1978, based on several years experience. He felt that relations were at a very low point, damaged primarily by the negotiations for fiscal arrangements in the 1960s (especially for shared cost programs, such as medicare), as well as those for constitutional reform, which began toward the end of the seventies. This had resulted in "une détérioration sérieuse du climat de confiance réciproque" (Bernard, 1979). Several federal initiatives continue to cause ill-feelings within the provincial governments. Premier Grant Devine of Saskatchewan, in a statement following the 1983 premiers' conference, asserted that he was disturbed by the federal government's apparent willingness to take a unilateral approach to the issue of health-care funding; he found this to be inconsistent with the spirit of ongoing cooperation between the two levels of government that the prime minister had urged the premiers to continue. Then there is the perennially vexatious issue of oil pricing — always with us — in which the interests of the producing provinces are different from those of the industrialized and populous, consuming ones. The federal government is virtually compelled to take a position, which is likely to be perceived as "unilateral" by both sides.

Bilateral Meetings

There was only one first ministers' conference in 1983 (in March), and that was concerned with constitutional aboriginal matters. The Constitution of Canada, given royal assent in April 1982, required that such a conference be convened within one year. The most recent first ministers' conference on the economy was held in January 1982. That was generally considered to be a failure. It is remembered primarily for Prime Minister

Trudeau's assertion that "cooperative federalism is dead." The previous meeting on the economy had been held in 1978.

At the end of 1983, Giles Gherson of *The Financial Post* wrote:

> These days, the federal government is striving to avoid situations which could provoke confrontation with all the provinces at once. The new approach is to bilateralize federal-provincial relations in the hope bargaining one-on-one can avoid transforming essentially manageable issues into major constitutional power struggles.[8]

In 1978, the Alberta government proposed that an annual first ministers' conference on the economy be entrenched in the Constitution.[9] A communiqué from the provincial premiers' conference in August 1983 advocated that one-on-one encounters with the prime minister be held in the various provincial capitals. The premiers' attitudes too had changed: they were wary lest a first ministers' conference be used by the federal government as part of an election campaign.

Decline in Conflict

Despite these various trends away from cooperative federalism, there have been some important recent positive developments in federal-provincial relations. Major bilateral agreements were reached in 1983, including new oil and gas pricing accords with Alberta and Saskatchewan to allow for declining world oil prices. Significant agreements were signed, as well, with the provinces of Newfoundland and Nova Scotia with respect to the restructuring of the fishery sector. Despite the increasing tendency for the federal government to fund projects alone, bilateral shared-cost agreements continued to be signed between Ottawa and the ten provincial governments, providing for various public works projects, often in regions of high unemployment, as part of job creation schemes.

The recession was one factor contributing to the reduction in conflict in federal-provincial relations. In a sense, it forced governments to work together. There was similarity in the fiscal policies and the budgets of the various governments, a result of having to deal with problems of restraint in the face of the recession. There was a concerted effort to develop fiscal policies that did not conflict. Throughout 1983 there were renewed calls for cooperation from both orders of government, especially in economic policy. By coordinating federal and provincial budgets and fiscal policies, all governments sought to attain common economic goals. Furthermore, given the fragile nature of the economy, there was the need to instil investor and consumer confidence.

The Western premiers held a meeting on February 2, 1983 and urged better federal-provincial cooperation in the battle against unemployment and the recession. They sensed a new willingness on the part of the federal government to work with the provinces.[10]

During the fiscal year 1982–83, the federal and provincial finance ministers held three meetings. The participants agreed that these were more conciliatory than previous encounters; all recognized the need to work together. Prince Edward Island stated:

> The atmosphere of these meetings has been much less tense than those of the preceding year and a significant degree of consensus has emerged on many of the economic and financial issues which were discussed.[11]

In a letter to the chairman of the premiers' conference in August 1983, Prime Minister Trudeau emphasized the importance of cooperation between the governments and the need for all of them to work together to improve economic conditions. He wrote:

> The government of Canada is determined to pursue its search for a more effective mix of economic policies and to do so in close cooperation with provincial governments as well as business and labour organizations. . . . We do not think that we have all the answers.[12]

Although condemned by some of the premiers as "mere politicking," others felt that Ottawa was genuinely interested in the views of the provincial governments with regard to economic policy.

There were a number of appeals, primarily from the provinces, for renewed cooperation between federal and provincial governments. In a 1983 document, the Alberta government called for a return to consultation and cooperation.[13] It argued that the economic growth of the country depended on the governments working together in an atmosphere of stability and trust. The same theme was voiced at the annual premiers' conference.

Another way in which the economic recession of 1981–83 may have helped to reduce the conflict and tension that had been so prevalent in intergovernmental relations in recent years was by shifting the resources and priorities of governments and Canadians generally. All governments had been preoccupied by economic problems. They had been drained of much of their fighting spirit. Generally, federal-provincial jurisdictional battles were laid aside. The economy dominated the public agenda, and the resources of all governments were focussed on the recession. Jeffrey Simpson wrote:

> All is quiet, however, temporarily, on the federal-provincial front. Both sides — to say nothing of the public — are exhausted from the patriation struggle. Recession has grounded the high-flying aspirations of assertive provinces.[14]

The recession had taken its toll on the population of Canada as well. As Premier Davis of Ontario asserted, "The public is a little tired of confrontation." It was generally felt that the electorate wanted the two levels of government to cooperate and work together.

The effect of the recession on tempering the attitudes of the various governments toward one another was bolstered by the prevalent feeling that a federal election would soon be held. There was some evidence that in some policy areas, the provinces had decided to wait out the Liberal government.

The opposition Progressive Conservatives held a substantial lead in popular opinion polls throughout 1983, and to many a change in government at the federal level seemed inevitable. It was generally believed that most of the provincial premiers would have preferred to deal with the federal Progressive Conservative party (seven of the ten provincial governments were Conservative, an eighth was Social Credit and Quebec had its Parti Québécois government). Also, intergovernmental relations had suffered under the turbulent Trudeau years, resulting in a worsening of relations brought on largely by the attitudes of the new federalism.

This stance by the provinces was enhanced with the election of Brian Mulroney as the leader of the federal Conservative party. Many of the provincial premiers seemed to think they could reach better understandings with him than they could with the Liberal government. This belief was fostered by the position of the Liberal party in the past on matters such as offshore oil and transfer payments. As well, statements by Mr. Mulroney, asserting his determination to renew cooperative federalism, were encouraging to the provinces. The question was left in abeyance with Mr. Trudeau's resignation, the choice of John Turner as party leader and prime minister, and the calling of a federal election for September 4, 1984. The Conservative victory opens the door to a new set of federal-provincial relationships.

It is premature to speculate at length on the prospects. It is still not known whether the tension in federal-provincial relations of the later Trudeau years, or the relative harmony of the Pearson period of cooperative federalism, is the normal relationship. And we do not know whether an improvement in the economic performance of the country will bring a return of tension or a new period of good feelings. Much will depend on the regional impact of the changes. Even more will turn on the attitudes of government leaders and on their willingness to make changes in both institutional structures and policies. Of course, the relationship between Quebec and Ottawa is basic — and that turns on a number of factors.

Developments on the federal-provincial front may have implications for interaction between governments and interest groups. It can be that when relations between the two orders of government are poor, nongovernmental interests, especially business, are more likely to be consulted seriously as part of the policy-making process. One government may view certain interest groups as allies in its battle with another. Furthermore, when making unilateral policy decisions and, therefore, bypassing the other order of government, a government may be more likely to look to interest groups for input.

During the last few years of the Trudeau regime, there is some evidence that these developments were taking place. In the debate over Bill S-31, for example, interest groups lined up behind either the federal or the Quebec government, depending on where their interests lay. The federal government's policy over the Crow Rate was based, in large part, on the recommendations of the Gilson task force; this body elicited input from groups and citizens in society. The provincial governments were not consulted.

The implications for the future are unclear. A major concern for newly elected Prime Minister Brian Mulroney has been the restoration of cooperation between the federal and provincial governments. If the position of interest groups is enhanced during periods of acrimonious federal-provincial relations, could it be that interest groups would be harmed by a return to an era of good relations among the governments? Mulroney has promised to include *both* provincial government *and* interest groups in the development of a national consensus. It remains to be seen if the nurturing of one of these relationships necessarily occurs at the expense of the other.

Chapter 4

Interest Groups and the Division of Powers

What are the current issues and problems relating to the relationship of groups with governments in the federal state? What is the impact of the division of powers on groups? How much are group behaviour and the structuring of the groups forced to conform to the realities of divided jurisdiction? What effect does the action of groups have on the working of the federal system? Can we use theoretical formulations to explain how groups influence government, or are frustrated in their attempts, in a federal setting? How do groups affect the balance of power between provincial and federal levels of government? How do their actions affect intergovernmental relations, and how are they involved in that process?

Effect on Groups

If one accepts the claim that the potential for influencing public policy depends in part on an interest group's structure, functioning and access to decision makers, then the division of powers will affect the ability of a pressure group to accomplish this end. To attain access to government, pressure groups must accommodate themselves to the way in which power is organized within the political system. (This is particularly true in Canada, where no serious attempts have been made to formalize the role of private interests in the policy-making process.) The process of accommodation in turn affects the structure and functioning of the group. Federalism has a great impact in determining the structural features of Canadian life. The inherent tension that exists between the dynamic of federalism and that of interest group politics automatically involves pressure groups in situations of tension. "The political language of federalism, a language for conducting competition and cooperation between territorially based groups and their governments, is necessarily hostile to the nationwide politics of class'' (Cairns, 1977, p. 719). Federalism throws up barriers to the combination and recombination of individuals in the pursuit of functional interests by placing certain territorially defined interests outside the play of open competition with the other interests of society. For example, French-Canadians in Quebec can rely on the constitutional authority of the provincial government to protect French-Canadian concerns, rather than having to fight for government recognition along with the minority cultural groups in Canada. On this basis, a shift toward a more pluralistic society could threaten the political stability of a country like Canada, where special recognition of regional integrity has been crucial in securing the continued support within Quebec for Confederation.

Similarly, the different perceptions of the public interest held by the federal and provincial governments create difficulties for the smooth functioning of interest groups:

> The political incentives for the federal government to couch its claims in the language of individual citizens' rights and obligations engender a direct conflict with provincial claims on behalf of territorially-based communities, the reconciliation of which is worked out in the federal process. (ibid., p. 718)

Paul Pross proposes that political communities can shape individually distinctive provincial political systems; this, in turn, influences the mode and characteristics of pressure groups within that political system (Pross, 1976, p. 132).

> Even where constitutional forms are consistent — as they are across the provinces — there is good reason to think that distinctive provincial political climates may condition the kind of legitimacy and opportunities for influence which are central to group politics.   (Chandler and Chandler, 1979, p. 72)

A survey of the effects of political cultures in different parts of the country reveals significant regional variations: group activity has been relatively low in the Atlantic provinces in the past, since the traditional patronage-based party system has withstood the pressure to move toward a meritocratic system that normally accompanies the rise of the bureaucratic state (although there are signs that this is now changing). Group-based politics has developed only fairly recently in Quebec, where the Church and party have been the chief agents for articulating values. There remains a residual feeling that interest groups are an illegitimate means of participating in the political system. Ontario, on the other hand, has a strong group environment where institutionalized and issue-oriented groups flourish; and the West has a dynamic group life. In British Columbia the groups are seen as hostile to one another, and highly competitive; in the Prairie provinces, interest groups are seen as representatives of shared community values (Pross, 1976, pp. 139–40).

Participation in federal political life exercises a pull away from regional particularisms for those involved:

In other words, in each of the provinces pressure group behaviour will exhibit a continuing tension between the pull toward national patterns exercised by the federal government and the more idiosyncratic behaviour required of those who take part in provincial politics. (ibid., p. 132)

The competition between defining interests in terms of community and defining them in the abstract language of rights can be particularly serious for interest groups when this conflict reveals itself within the structure of a single group. In Canada, this has been true of a number of national organizations whose constituent unit in Quebec prefers to affiliate its interests with the province instead of the nation as a whole:

During a period when the division of functions between the two levels of government is a matter of controversy, organizations including important elements from the two cultural communities are subjected to severe internal strains when French Canadians from Quebec wish their province to have exclusive powers to deal with affairs which other Canadians see as appropriate objectives of federal action. (Smiley, 1970, p. 125)

For many Québécois and their associations, a major concern is to defend and protect the rights, institutions and practices of French-speaking Québécois, especially in relation to language, education, religion and culture. This has led to the formation of many "parallel associations" functioning in the French language but concerned with the same substantive area of interest as the "national," or so-called bilingual, association. This has occurred, especially since the quickening of Québécois self-awareness in the sixties, in areas where the national association had become de facto an English-language one, while usually affecting bilingualism. The French-speaking element was always a minority, and it often found its views outvoted or passed over by the English-speaking majority. This frustration produced protests and in many cases led either to the splitting into two associations (one English-speaking and the other French-), or more often, the setting up of a new, separate French-speaking association to express Québécois concerns. The older "bilingual," "national" association usually remained, claiming to continue to speak for both language groups in the field concerned. This tendency for separate Québécois associations to be formed was particularly common in the academic learned societies, in the trade union movement, and in business organizations such as the Conseil du patronat du Québec and the Chambre de commerce du Québec, as well as in agricultural and professional associations. Even when no separate Quebec association was formed, the Quebec section of the national association usually was granted or assumed greater autonomy than the other regional groupings — and of course normally it would function in French.

Separate organizations for the francophones seemed the only way to overcome with certainty the underrepresentation in "national" organizations, which typically amounted to about 10 percent of executive positions compared to about 28 percent of the Canadian population (Bernard, 1977, p. 263). This underrepresentation is largely traceable to lower levels of participation in voluntary associations by francophones and to their underrepresentation in the business world generally. Finally, it is also attributable to the fact that they now tend to join the francophone rather than the "national" organization. To counter the tendency of the "national" associations to claim to speak for the whole country, and also to make their own, often different, positions heard, the francophones have gone a long way in setting up parallel francophone organizations.

Once in place, these francophone groups are inclined to develop closer relationships with the Quebec government than with Ottawa. This is especially true in areas where the relevant jurisdiction is provincial. This pressure on the Quebec government is inclined to push it further along the road to autonomy (ibid., pp. 263–66).

A good example is the role of the women's lobby in the constitutional debates of 1980–81. One participant, Chaviva Hosek, claims that it was very difficult to establish a consensus for unified action because "women were residents of different provinces with various political party affiliations and different views on patriation" (Hosek, 1983, p. 283). Women in Quebec wanted the provinces to have control over civil rights because they perceived the government in Quebec as forward-looking on many issues of concern to women; whereas women in English-speaking Canada were motivated to support federal control in this area by their view of a lack of sensitivity toward women's issues shown by provincial premiers in the rest of the country. One can say that, in general, federalism is a crosscutting force to the usual dynamics of the interest group process (although we shall see later that groups do try to capitalize on the situation). By imposing one form of collective action (based on territory) upon another (based on functional, pluralist competition), federalism increases the external and internal tensions that would be much less for interest groups in a unitary system. These features are now examined.

The simple fact that there is a division of powers has an effect on the formation of interest groups. Pross observes that institutionalized groups dominate at the federal level, while both issue-oriented groups and institutionalized groups operate at the provincial level. Institutionalized groups sometimes locate at the provincial level in response to political and economic realities (e.g., the oil industry in Alberta); but issue-oriented groups are attracted to the provincial level by a number of structural factors:

. . . the constitutional responsibility, the physical proximity and the relatively undifferentiated nature of provincial administration [which] provide a more hospitable setting for groups with a weak organizational policy structure.

(Pross, 1976, p. 135)

Thus, the existence of smaller, regional political units has encouraged the development of issue-oriented groups, which lack the resources necessary to establish permanent relations at the federal level. This has not stopped them from petitioning the federal government to intervene in situations where provincial attitudes were obstructing their interests. For example, health coalitions from around the country used the Breau task force on fiscal federalism as a vehicle for requesting that the federal government force the hand of provincial governments on the issue of extra-billing and user fees. Also, groups on both sides of the abortion and capital punishment issues have pressured both levels of government. Such actions have been enhanced by the development of more open and formalized structures for group input at the federal level. In recent years, the federal government has shown a desire to develop new mechanisms of consultation and to expand existing ones. This linkage between the centre and sub-provincial networks could have some interesting implications for national integration. The tendency for issue-oriented groups to define their interests in functional terms and to emphasize individual rights against the state lends support to the federal (Liberal) government's recent atomistic view of society. Second, linkages between the federal government and community organizations bypass the provinces without necessarily destroying regional identities. This direct federal link with the regions at the local level could encourage decentralization beyond the provincial level, despite the constitutional division of powers. The Charter of Rights and Freedoms has opened the door to greater group activity.

The manner in which powers are distributed between the two orders of government is very important to the fate of pressure groups and their interests. David Kwavnick offers the example of the Canadian Union of Students to demonstrate his claim that "the strength and cohesion of interest groups will tend to mirror the strength in the particular area of government to which they enjoy access" (Kwavnick, 1975, p. 72). The direct subsidization of universities by the federal government led, in 1951, to the reorganization of the National Federation of Canadian University Students as the Canadian Union of Students (CUS) in 1964. This new body was located in Ottawa, the source of university funding. However, in 1966 Ottawa decided to route university funding through the provinces, and by 1968 the CUS was in ruins; in 1969 it collapsed, because there was nothing left for it to do.

A shift in the division of powers can affect not only the structure and functioning of a group, but can seriously undermine its interests. A constitutional meeting held in February 1979 almost resulted in the transfer of jurisdiction over divorce to provincial governments. Had this shift in powers taken place, it would have had severely uneven and in some provinces inequitable consequences for women. The enforcement of custody and maintenance would become extremely difficult because of variations in provincial legislation. During the process of patriation of the Constitution, this incident served as a "symbolic reminder of what could happen to women's interests when no informed women sat at the table where political deals between first ministers were struck" (Hosek, 1983, p. 284).

A most important development in the distribution of powers to affect interest groups has been the advent of cooperative federalism after the Second World War. Prior to the 1940s, when a more classical style of federalism prevailed, groups clustered around the level of government with jurisdiction over their interests and whose policies most affected them. Only those interest groups involved in areas of concurrent jurisdiction found it necessary to maintain effective federal and provincial organizations. That pattern has changed primarily as a consequence of Canada's "attempt to achieve the benefits of the positive state under the aegis of cooperative federalism" (Pross, 1976, p. 141). As Kwavnick's example of the Canadian Union of Students shows, "a few groups have suffered sharp reversals of fortune as jurisdictional accommodation was worked out" (ibid.).

Most groups have adjusted to the new and complex structures developed to accommodate federal-provincial cooperation. The shift from classical federalism to an emphasis on intergovernmental relations has resulted in new forms of interest group behaviour as they adapted to the new arrangements. The number of groups increased, as many existing institutionalized groups adopted federal structures in order to be prepared to deal with both levels of government. Provincial organizations established national headquarters, and national organizations set up constituent units in the provinces. However, Alan Cairns observes that most national organizations operate as confederations despite their federal structure:

> The [provincial units] reflect the local concerns of their members who often identify with the provincial agency which administers the provincial policies affecting them. As a result, the national executive is sometimes reduced to an aggregation of contradictory provincial particularisms unable to agree on a position towards proposed Ottawa policies.   (Cairns, 1977, p. 714)

Helen Jones Dawson identifies the contradiction faced by federal groups. While they depend on the support of their provincial clientele for their membership base, to move too far to accommodate them would make the formulation of national policy impossible:

> Thus, many national pressure groups are frequently confronted with the following paradox: if a provincial organization permits its policies to be too profoundly influenced by national as opposed to local considerations, it will lose support among its local clientele, and this in turn will diminish the national organization's political impact; whereas if the provincial organizations adhere too rigidly to the policies approved at the local level, it may be impossible to achieve any kind of national policy at all.   (Dawson, 1975, p. 31)

This problem poses less difficulty for groups whose interests fall under provincial jurisdiction, but it can create serious difficulties for national organizations attempting to influence policy at the federal level. This situation is exacerbated by the fact that provincial units will at times by-pass the national organization and appeal directly to the minister from that region, or ask provincial governments to use their influence on the federal government on an issue. These actions have the advantage of expanding the group's contacts with government, but they also undermine the authority of the national organization in representing its membership.

The confusion over jurisdictional responsibility that has resulted from cooperative federalism is another source of difficulty for pressure groups. Garth Stevenson has argued that one effect of federalism is to keep many issues out of the national arena, especially class conflict, since its elements are class controlled. This may work in the way that Dawson suggests:

> Perhaps the pressure groups find that the most frustrating political outcome of the Canadian constitutional structure is the fact that both the federal and provincial governments often justify inaction on the grounds that each lacks jurisdiction. (ibid., p. 32)

Interest groups at times damage their position with both levels of government by showing insensitivity, or simply ignorance, of the constitutional realities of the system. Jurisdictional disputes between governments can take years to settle. In the meantime, uncertainty can exacerbate regional tensions within groups that reflect the differences in attitudes between governments. When issues are resolved, the decision may necessitate the reorganization or even the demise of the group. The absence of uniform legislation (as in the area of labour law) can also affect group cohesion. As the constituent units focus on different circumstances, they develop different sets of interests, which may make consensus hard to achieve. Unlike Canadian political parties, pressure groups cannot overcome federal tensions by the separation of federal and provincial associations, owing to their lack of resources and institutionalization. (Cairns, 1977, p. 714).

The development of cooperative federalism and later executive federalism have tended to place greater strains on the financial resources of interest groups. Since groups must be prepared to respond to either level of government, they must maintain well-staffed offices at two levels or risk losing influence. This means that groups have fewer resources to devote to performing their social functions, which are important for maintaining group cohesion. Perhaps even more important, there is less money to pay experts to prepare high quality briefs advocating their policy proposals. If Hugh Faulkner is correct in his assessment that good management is now the most crucial factor in participating successfully in the policy-making process (and not the absolute amount of money available), then the advent of cooperative federalism has diminished the effective influence of pressure groups by increasing the load they have to carry (Faulkner, 1975, p. 252). Interest groups have basically two choices for overcoming these difficulties: curtailing their activity at the national level, or seeking government funding. Unlike the small citizens' groups that have proliferated since the 1960s, established groups have been very reluctant, perhaps justifiably, to accept government funding for fear that the national office will be coopted. Helen Jones Dawson observes:

> Financial problems may help to explain one of the distinctive features of the Canadian groups, and that is their attitude toward national headquarters. There is a reluctance to have a national office at all, more than reluctance to locate it in Ottawa, and determination to keep it small and poor.
>
> (Dawson, 1975, pp. 33–34)

While this attitude seems contrary to the better interests of the groups involved, it may reflect their sense of increased powerlessness within the political system. The formalization of policy-making structures for deciding jurisdictional issues has not been accompanied by a formalized role for established interests.

In general, cooperative federalism has complicated and confused the tasks of interest groups by requiring that they do too much at both levels. While interest groups may have "adjusted" to the more pragmatic approach taken by governments toward the formal division of powers, their incremental, ad hoc approach does not help them in dealing with a system geared toward the coordination of broad policy objectives. If future governments manage to achieve some degree of disentanglement (as certain aspiring leaders have proposed), perhaps interest groups in a few areas will be able to avoid some of the problems associated with government interdependence.

The fact that groups are called upon now to do more at both levels of government affects the power relations between groups. Rich institutionalized groups and large business corporations are easily able to meet the financial costs of greater representational efforts and the need to acquire sophisticated expertise. This gives them a greater advantage than before over the poorer groups, particularly the single-issue citizen groups, which cannot follow them down the road of greater expenditure.

Groups' Effect on the Division of Powers

The Multiple-Crack Explanation

While it is true that the onus is initially on interest groups to adapt to the structures of policy making, it is almost inevitable that once involved in the process, "governmental institutions will be shaped by as well as shape the structures and activities of interest groups" (Smiley, 1980, p. 148). The paradigm of interest group interaction with the federal system of government that has formed the basis of the debate in the Canadian literature has largely beeen the multiple-crack explanation.

This perception was originally developed by Morton Grodzin to describe the relationship between interest groups and federalism in the American political system. Canadian political scientists have become convinced of its application in the Canadian context by drawing a rather questionable comparison between the American separation of powers and Canadian division of powers. This tendency is epitomized by Cairns' comment about the "Canadian version of the separation of powers":

> The dynamics and weaknesses of political federalism are rendered more explicable if it is recognized that we have stumbled into a peculiar Canadian version of the American separation of powers. The reaching of agreement on the innumerable major issues which clog the federal-provincial agenda requires the approval of independent political authorities with distinct, and separate bases of electoral, party, group and bureaucratic support. They are not constitutionally beholden to each other and they are aligned with large and powerful constituencies of interests that can be mobilized behind the evocative labels of provincial rights and the national interest. Indeed, the Canadian version of the separation of powers may be more difficult to work than its American counterpart, for it involves not just the separate legislative and executive strata of the policy-making process but governments, conscious of their historical position, jealous of the prerogatives and aggressively enterprising in the performance of their managerial responsibilities for their societies.
>
> (Cairns, 1977, p. 724)

Grodzin's thesis contends that the richer pressure groups, which can stand the costs, particularly value the federal system because the existence of two levels of government provides them with multiple access points to pursue their policy objectives. Eventually, pressure groups gravitate to the level of government most receptive to their demands and constitutionally most able to accede to them. For the groups, the value of the federal division of powers is that if they fail to achieve their goals at one level, they can seek satisfaction from the other level of government. Grodzin's "crack" not only means many access points but more opportunities to exert pressure on government. A negative impact of federal systems is their effect on group cohesion; if the group maintains a corresponding federal structure to maximize its access to power holders, it will tend to scatter its resources and personnel. This diminishes its ability to articulate and defend its goals (Schultz, 1977, pp. 375–76). First, groups must meet this challenge by incurring the higher costs involved in exerting pressure at more than one level of government. This also imposes greater strain on the organizational structure of the group to coordinate and orchestrate its campaigns in different places at the same time. On the other hand, Presthus argues, the division of powers in Canada enables interest groups to penetrate and influence the national political system by providing them with alternative centres of power and different avenues of access (Presthus, 1971, p. 446). Second, the challenge to the groups is greater. The richer and more competently led ones will be enhanced, and the poorer and less ably directed ones will be outdistanced; but the more access points there are, the more vulnerable is government to pressure.

The underlying premise of this model is its acceptance of the liberal democratic state as a neutral instrument for the aggregation of public interests and demands. From this basis flows the assumption that interest groups are able to distance themselves from the political machinery and maintain their independence in the pursuit of policy objectives. This, in turn, supports the claim that groups can play one level of government off against the other, as competition occurs between governments for the information, status, legitimacy, etc. that interest groups have to offer.

Evidence for the multiple-crack theory has been found in case studies by Kwavnick, Bucovetsky and Schultz. Kwavnick's study uses the conflict between the Canadian Labour Congress (CLC) and the Confederation of National Trade Unions (CNTU) to demonstrate that rival groups representing the same interests but having access to different levels of government in a federal system will attempt to shift power to the level of government to which they enjoy access (Kwavnick, 1975, p. 84). This research shows that the Quebec-based CNTU attempted to weaken the federal government in order to strengthen the position of provincial governments, while the CLC has been persistent in its demand that major questions such as social security, taxation, education and labour relations, be declared of general interest to all Canadians and brought under federal jurisdiction.

M.W. Bucovetsky shows how the mining industry was successful in mobilizing provincial governments against the proposal of the Carter Commission on taxation to eliminate generous tax concessions enjoyed by the extractive industries. His study demonstrates the way in which regional centres of support can aid interest groups where they are effective in first convincing provincial authorities of the merits of their cause:

> The mining and petroleum industries can bring intense political pressure to bear because mining shapes so many regionally distinct communities. Where mining exists, it tends to dominate. At the same time, the federal character of the constitution, the national diffusion of the industry and its common viewpoint on federal tax policy increase the number of political pressure points on which local influence can be brought to bear. (Bucovetsky, 1975, p. 105).

By offering to support one order of government as opposed to another, pressure groups can enhance a government's "legitimacy" to act in an area outside its own jurisdiction. Thus, the mining industry took advantage of its crucial role in the economies of the provinces, especially in the West, to further the bargaining power of the provincial governments affecting federal taxation legislation (Schwartz, 1978, p. 331).

Recent events reveal the reverse situation also occurring. The support of the appeals of health and social welfare groups from across the country reinforced the federal government's claim that medicare was a national concern and legitimized federal legislation penalizing those provinces that allowed doctors to extra-bill, and hospitals to impose user fees.

Richard Schultz describes the behaviour of the Canadian Trucking Association (CTA) prior to 1965 as typical of the multiple-crack thesis. Because of the long-standing belief that the federal government was biased in favour of the transportation system, which it regulated, viz., rail transportation, the CTA has long sought to ensure that responsibility for truck transport belongs to the provinces. However, when attempts failed to have the provinces establish uniform regulations, and when joint hearings were ignored by the provinces, the CTA utilized the opportunity afforded it by the federal system. It petitioned the federal government to change the legislation delegating regulatory power to the provinces:

> The industry has supported that level of government which was assumed to be the more responsive to its demands, and then had sought to maintain what was viewed as a beneficient constitutional *status quo*. Only when this beneficence became dubious did the industry deviate from its traditional posture, and then only to request the federal government to force the provinces to do what they would not do voluntarily.   (Schultz, 1977, p. 379)

Similarly, Alan Cairns explains how business is able to play one province off against another in order to establish the most favourable environment:

> Capital knows no loyalty. Its easy mobility across provincial and national boundaries exerts a strong pressure on each province not to deviate in its tax system from the other provincial systems with which it is in unavoidable competition, and on Canada not to impose a more burdensome or discriminatory system of taxes than exists in the U.S.   (Cairns, 1977, pp. 711–12)

Cairns gives the example of big business in British Columbia, which relies on the election threat that an NDP government may dry up investment.

We do not yet know how widespread or how effective this type of behaviour is, or the conditions under which it occurs. The literature suggests that the incidence of this type of behaviour is infrequent and uncertain in its success. This can be related to one of the basic criticisms of the multiple-crack thesis. Its proponents tend to confuse access with influence — a link that often cannot be made. But if access equals influence, then to maximize influence, groups must maximize access. As Whittington and Van Loon observe, increasing points of access may result in groups spreading their resources too thinly, thus reducing influence. This is another way of saying that interest groups must make trade-offs between concentrating their efforts on particular decision makers and reaching a maximum number of decision makers. And, of course, it ignores the differences in funds available to some groups compared to others. More research could test this hypothesis.

Probably this trade-off is easier when the relevant jurisdictional responsibility belongs to only one level of government. Dawson, in fact, notes that organizations representing a clientele mainly affected by provincial laws do not maintain close contact with the federal government. As a result, when federal legislation affects them they find it difficult to exert influence at that level (Dawson, 1975, p. 32). This, in turn, reinforces their ties with the provincial level of government.

Why do such attempts occur? Case studies suggest that they arise only after group attempts at influence have been frustrated at one level. Thus, in general it appears that when a group is seen to lobby a government about an issue for which it does not have direct and primary jurisdiction, then most likely it has lost its battle at the other level of government. To the extent that this loss represents the victory of opposing interest groups at the provincial level, it can be argued that a by-product of group conflict at the provincial level may be the transformation of the issues at stake into intergovernmental ones.

The literature indicates that the success of this strategy will vary, depending on the extent to which the issue can be presented as belonging to the other level of government. This may or may not be a very difficult task to perform. Usually some jurisdictional peg can be found on which to hang an appeal for action by one level of government against another. Cairns notes that the shift from classifical to cooperative federalism has marked a change in interest group tactics. Whereas J.R. Mallory records the way economic interests used to resort to litigation to weaken the constitutional legitimacy of government to regulate them, Pierre Trudeau observes that interest groups have at times attempted to take advantage of jurisdictional confusion to try to convince governments to act on their behalf (Cairns,1977, p. 712).

Recently Canadian governments are growing increasingly reluctant to enter into new fields of jurisdiction where potential revenues do not exceed projected costs. Also, governments at both levels appear to be more and more concerned to preserve their jurisdictional prerogatives. Therefore, opposition to the expansion of policy into new fields is becoming much riskier, and governments are increasingly unlikely to act simply to gain interest group support.

Generally, interaction leads to influence by affected groups only to the extent that the interest group demands coincide with and complement the bargaining strategies and objectives of the governments involved. If a group's support can enhance a government's strategy and help it realize its objectives, the government has an incentive for allying with it to the degree of the perceived enhancement or threat. Bucovetsky concludes from his analysis of the mining industry that, despite the successful pressure that interest groups induced provincial governments to bring on their behalf at the federal level, the real victor was the provinces "whose success in thwarting Ottawa confirmed the dependent, client status of the extractive industries at the provincial level, subsequently evidenced by heavy provincial tax and royalty increases" (Bucovetsky, 1975, pp. 108–109).

The other side of this situation is that a level of government may be reluctant to lose interest group support or incur interest group opposition. Out of this concern arises another obstacle to groups seeking to exploit the multiple cracks of the federal system: the degree to which groups fear that governments may retaliate against a group for defecting, or will try to neutralize its appeal made to the other level. In Schultz's analysis, both these tactics were employed by provincial governments anxious to retain the Canadian Trucking Association's support for provincial regulation of the trucking industry. Although incentives were offered to the CTA, sanctions were threatened too. As well, the Quebec government attempted to exacerbate regional divisions between the Quebec provincial association and the national body. The result was an "embarrassing nonconformity," which undermined the effectiveness of the CTA's support for federal regulation of trucking. Generally, one cannot overemphasize that the recent concentration through the creation of central agencies — of both federal and provincial governments — has lessened dramatically the possible impact of pressure groups' attempts to change government policy once formulated; hence, group concern to be consulted at the policy-formulation stage.

The experience of the groups in these two studies raises doubts as to the appropriateness of the multiple-crack thesis in the Canadian context. Simeon and Schultz have levelled criticisms at the model for its failure to explain adequately interest group behaviour in areas of governmental relations, especially since the advent of cooperative federalism in the fifties. Their views are discussed below. However, the multiple-crack theory still remains the preferred point of reference for understanding interest group behaviour in the federal system. For example, Schultz states his view as falling between the extremes of the multiple-crack thesis, which claims that there are no governmental constraints on the ability of groups to maximize the number of access points, and Richard Simeon's claim that, in cases with a federal-provincial dimension, interest groups tend to be frozen out of the process. Neither author questions whether the multiple-crack theory should have been used in the first place.

After all, the theory was designed to explain a political system based on the separation of powers, where groups deal with functionally defined, institutionally entrenched agencies responsible for a specific aspect of the entire policy-making process. To draw an analogy between this U.S. situation and the Canadian, in which economic interdependence has forced both orders of government, to some extent at least, to coordinate their actions, is to apply the theory to very different circumstances.

The impact on interest groups caused by the rise of the social service state and the centralization of power within the executive, is just as important to understanding the nature of interest group involvement in the intergovernmental arena as is the rise of executive federalism. It beckons groups into the policy-making nexus because there is now so much at stake, but it also makes the task of groups in seeking to influence policy very much more difficult.

The Balance of Power

The position of interest groups in relation to the balance of power between the federal and provincial governments is a key theme in the literature. J.A. Corry commented in 1958:

> . . . in these democratic aggregates with which we are concerned, sentiment and opinion, molded and canalized no doubt by material factors, will decide where power lies. Because power alone can balance power, the provinces and states have to keep strong and vigorous bodies of opinion on their side if they are able to stop the aggrandizement of national governments.
>
> (Corry, 1958, p. 115)

This comment reflects the confidence in the dynamic power of the federal government that was general in the postwar period. Then, all agreed that the emergence during the war of national elites was bound to cause centralization of power in Ottawa, with the concomitant subordination of the provinces. Few predicted the rise of militant demands in Quebec for recognition, but Corry did recognize that certain regionally located interests could lead to decentralization:

> Those whose interests are concentrated on the development and exploitation of the natural resources of a single province naturally want the federal government to leave them alone while they cultivate the good will of the provincial government.
>
> (ibid., p. 114)

Donald Smiley addressed the importance of interest group alignment to the survival of the federal system:

> If most of the influential groups in any federation came to look exclusively to either one level of government or the other, it is not likely that federalism could long survive. . . .
>
> (Smiley, 1970, p. 6)

Likewise, the degree to which interests are defined either regionally or functionally will influence the balance of power between the federal government and the provinces. Kwavnick suggests that groups can perform as agents for the integration or disintegration of the federal political system:

> . . . to the extent that interest groups, like other voluntary organizations, are agents of socialization serving to orient their members and the general public toward the level of government to which their demands are directed, it would appear that both the centralization and the disintegration of a federal political system, once begun and other factors remaining unchanged, are self-sustaining processes.
>
> (Kwavnick, 1975, p. 83)

The closest example of this situation is the case of Quebec, where many branch associations have withdrawn from national ones to establish their own independent organizations (for example, the labour movement). This phenomenon is particularly relevant to understanding the development of separatist movements. Smiley observes a similarity between the circumstances in Quebec and the situation in the American South just before the Civil War (Smiley, 1970, p. 7). He conjectures that the successful operation of cooperative federalism requires a public whose attitudes are pragmatic as to the appropriate level of government for carrying out given responsibilities.

Kwavnick's statement does beg two questions. First, it applies only to the extent that groups serve as agents of socialization. Kwavnick argues that "groups organized on a local or regional basis will tend to strengthen local awareness, local loyalties and local particularisms, thus reinforcing fragmentation." Alternatively:

> . . . groups organized on a national basis will tend to strengthen the national awareness of their members, to create a feeling of indentification with the national institutions of government, to heighten feelings of efficacy and involvement with those institutions and thus promote national integration.
> (Kwavnick, 1975, p. 71)

For this claim to be valid it must be shown that the successful making of demands upon an order of government in the area of interest group concern, does in fact predispose individuals to support the expansion of that order into other fields of policy. Also, given the difficulty that national groups have in reconciling regional differences and arriving at a national consensus, it is not clear that national organizations are nearly as effective an instrument of national integration as the statement suggests.

The second question raised by Kwavnick's argument is that of infinite regression; that is, it shows how integration and disintegration operate once they are under way, but it offers no explanation as to what causes these processes to begin, or how they can be reversed. The implication is that the relationship between public support for government and shifts in the balance of power is purely linear and, therefore, irreversible. Surely, this relationship is more flexible; one would have to know what forces mobilize interests toward the centre or away from it.

But how can we understand why people's interests shift on questions of national significance? A better understanding of regionalism as an independent force within the country could certainly improve our knowledge of the relationship between society and government. One possible factor to consider is the country's external environment. Regardless of regional identities, most Canadians outside Quebec do identify with their country first and their province second (Simeon and Elkins, 1980). When the external environment poses a threat to the country as a whole, people broaden their parameters. During the 1940s, the experience of the war effort had a homogenizing effect on the attitudes of Canadians, supporting federal dominance. By the 1960s this sense of national community had worn down because of the increasingly apparent differences in political and economic interests among regions. Again, in the 1980s there are signs of at least a partial mobilization of the country in response to the deterioration of its international economic situation. Considering the present Royal Commission, it is interesting to note Smiley's speculation in 1970 about the possibility of a return of federal dominance:

> It is possible to imagine a situation where politically influential groups throughout Canada come to believe that decentralization of power was costing too much in terms of economic stability and growth.
>
> Some new federal political leadership might emerge which would successfully commit the country to a bold and popular programme of reform even in the opposition of the government of Quebec and perhaps the governments of some of the other provinces. (Smiley, 1970, p. 127)

Like the multiple-crack thesis, this interpretation of the impact of pressure groups on the balance of power implicitly suggests that the state is passive to its environment. However, it lends itself more readily to modification in response to the rise of the active (some would say *dirigiste*) state. Some analysts have claimed that governments now actively try to cultivate the political advantage to be gained through acquiring interest group support. Kwavnick expresses the major policy implication of the combination of these two factors:

> . . . one means by which a government in a federal political system may strengthen itself *vis-à-vis* government at the other level would be to encourage the development of as broad a range as possible of strong and cohesive private organizations dependent upon it. (Kwavnick, 1975, p. 84)

Similarly, Cairns supports the *dirigiste* view of the state when he attributes government self-interest as the primary motive behind the sponsoring of new groups: ". . . the deliberate creation and fostering by governments of interest groups, to whose induced demands they wish to respond, is a prime weapon for government survival in circumstances of aggressive intergovernmental competition (Cairns, 1977, pp. 716–17). The advantage of the balance of power approach is that it can make room for examining the dynamic interface between society and government. This is particularly important in Canada, where we have competition between powerful and independent elected governments.

Pressure Groups and Intergovernmental Relations

The multiple-crack thesis, designed to explain pressure group interaction with autonomous spheres of power, provides little basis for understanding the interdependence of governments that has arisen in Canada since the Second World War. The attempt to describe the relationship between pressure groups and intergovernmental relations in a situation where governments must coordinate their activities has led Simeon and Schultz to challenge the validity of the multiple-crack theory in the Canadian context. However, each takes a different approach and arrives at a different conclusion as to the role pressure groups play in the federal-provincial policy-making process. Simeon's analysis of the relationship between pressure groups and executive federalism leads him to conclude that despite the advantages groups might gain from a federal system in terms of general access to policy makers, the nature of Canadian federal-provincial relations is such that group participation tends to become severely restricted whenever an issue enters the intergovernmental arena (Simeon, 1972, p. 144).

He attributes this "freezing out" of interest groups to the operation of the policy-making process, which is designed primarily to accommodate the interests of governments. The rise of executive federalism as a forum for coordinating government actions has made governments the most important players in the process. The centralization of power at the executive level means that conflicts between governments are no longer diffused at the bureaucratic level but are channelled directly to cabinet. As a result, issues are now more politicized and public and, therefore, more intractable, as governments themselves seek to retain their powers and accomplish — and be seen to accomplish — broad policy objectives. The absence of formal mechanisms for interest group consultation means that governments have the discretionary power to exclude interest groups from the process, especially if group interests come into conflict with their own:

> Even if a government does act as a spokesman for a particular interest in the negotiations, these interests may be sacrificed. At best, interest group concerns will form only a part of a government's goals and, to the extent that they are less central than status or ideological goals, they will be the first to be jettisoned in the conference room. This will be especially true when there is great pressure to reach agreement. . . .   (ibid., p. 282)

Also, "the secrecy of the discussions means that group leaders may often be unaware of developments in federal-provincial negotiations which might involve them" (ibid., p. 144).

Chandler and Chandler also argue that federal-provincial relations are a unique policy-making setting where pressure groups are not very effective (Chandler and Chandler, 1979, p. 154). Glyn R. Berry also supports this view. In his study of the events leading up to the adoption of a national petroleum policy by the Trudeau government in 1973, he shows that prior to the energy crisis, the Western provinces and the federal National Energy Board had been "benevolently responsive" to the oil industry: ". . . government policy-making *vis-à-vis* energy had been a slow, deliberate process in which consultation with the industry was of paramount importance" (Berry, 1974, p. 632). However, once energy became an urgent political issue involving fundamental policy considerations, the industry seemed helpless to prevent measures that only a year before would have been seen by government as too radical. Politicization of the issue brought public scrutiny, which worked against the industry. As one oilman explained:

> The voluntary price freeze imposed by Prime Minister Trudeau could not, in all conscience, have been turned down by the industry which still bears the image of profiteering and monopoly formed in the public's mind way back in the days of the Standard Oil breakup. (ibid.)

Berry concludes that during a period of crisis, powerful interest groups will find their influence considerably reduced, and the situation is worsened when intensive federal-provincial bargaining is involved.

Schultz and Simeon agree on the basic point that the multiple-crack theory underestimates the costs involved for pressure groups that try to play off one government against another. However, Schultz has reservations about the frozen-out theory as well, since it neglects the important support function that pressure groups can provide in intergovernmental relations:

> Groups' support may be an important resource in the bargaining process, and consequently groups may play a much more extended and influential role in the process. (Schultz, 1977, p. 377)

Schultz points out that Simeon goes part way to recognizing this fact himself when he asserts that "political support is a scarce resource and participants compete for it, and the competition is part of the bargaining process" (Simeon and Dunn, 1982, p. 204). Schultz extends this statement further, suggesting that pressure group support as a variant of public support can be the object of intergovernmental competition.

The multiple-crack explanation and the frozen-out hypothesis both help to explain the impact of the political process on pressure groups, as determined by the institutional framework. In Simeon's case, it is the combination of the British parliamentary system and a federal division of powers that has determined the form that intergovernmental relations have taken in Canada; executive federalism, in turn, is responsible for restricting the participation of pressure groups in the policy-making process.

Schultz, on the other hand, is more concerned with outcomes. Central to his explanation is a *dirigiste* view of the state. In other words, he is more interested in the effect that the changing nature of the state has had on interest groups than in the impact of institutional changes that has accompanied it. The rise of the positive state is most important for the growth of powerful and active governments which consciously seek to shape their environment, of which interest groups are part. It is from this position that Schultz criticizes Grodzin and Simeon for assuming that the group-government relationship runs unilaterally from groups to government, whereas for Schultz the causal arrow should be seen as pointing in both directions to account also for the impact of government on groups:

> What appears to have been ignored in the literature is the role of governmental actors in fostering and exacerbating the potential for internal conflict for the purpose of exploiting group division in the intergovernmental arena. Furthermore, the "smacks" or "wallops" that Grodzin spoke of may be directed at the groups by government in an attempt to weaken the groups' ties with the other level of government. The purpose of such "cracks" is to undercut the political support claimed by a government in order to diminish its resources.
>
> (Schultz, 1977, p. 382)

Schultz demonstrates the validity of his position by examining the events that followed the decision of the Canadian Trucking Association (CTA) to reverse its traditional position and support the federal government's attempt to reclaim control over the regulation of truck transportation. By doing this, the CTA provoked severe provincial hostility, and in the intergovernmental conflict that ensued, the industry became the object of intense competition as both levels of government strove to gain industry support. At first, the CTA tried to resist the concerted efforts of the provinces to persuade the industry to no longer support the federal government. When pressure on Ottawa to implement the bill as soon as possible failed to bring results, however, the CTA eventually had to make its peace with the level of government in control of its immediate future. Thus, the provinces were able to undermine one of the major underpinnings for the federal government's new policy. Schultz concludes:

> The role of the CTA suggests that articulating and defending a position in terms of group demands may be a significant determinant of the nature and course of intergovernmental negotiations. Group support may be particularly effective as a resource if an actor can legitimize a course of action on the grounds that such a course is necessitated by a failure or inaction of the other level of government. (ibid., p. 393)

To support his claim that interest groups are not frozen-out, Schultz seeks to explain why Simeon's studies of the negotiation of fiscal arrangements and the Constitution showed little evidence of interest group involvement. He does this by asserting that these particular policy areas only involve the interests of governments and that, therefore, the governments themselves act as interest groups in these cases (Schultz, 1980, p. 171).

This analogy seems strained and disguises the fact that there is nothing about the nature of any intergovernmental issue that logically places it outside the sphere of pressure group interests. This is shown by the involvement of issue-oriented groups in recent fiscal relations and the constitutional debate. On the other hand, Simeon's study does not bar the possibility of governments using the political system to recruit interest group support. It merely shows that the process is biased in favour of the prerogatives of governments, rather than the insertion of interest group demands.

One reason for the lack of agreement about the nature of interest group involvement in the intergovernmental process must be the neglect of the role of public awareness in the analysis of the intergovernmental process. Glyn Berry's study reveals indirectly how public opinion can provide government with a legitimate excuse for dismissing interest group demands. But how would the situation have been resolved if public opinion had been strongly in favour of the oil industry? The difficult tasks of delineating the public interest and the interests of pressure groups, and studying how the two relate to each other and to the actions of governments, will have to be undertaken in the future if we are to achieve a greater understanding of the Canadian political system.

Both authors focus on intergovernmental relations as a unique process, and therefore do not locate the changes in the intergovernmental process within the context of broader changes in the Canadian political system. The recent involvement of issue-oriented groups in fiscal and constitutional negotiations is an indication of the fundamental connection beween changes in the role of pressure groups in the intergovernmental arena and the shift away from elite accommodation due to the rise of the active state and the changes in the decision-making process.

The same conditions that favoured elite accommodation at the general policy-making level up until the mid-1960s applied also to the intergovernmental arena. As long as provincial governments were interested only in short-term goals involving specific programs instead of long-range budgetary and program planning, major policy questions continued to be settled at the intergovernmental level. The conditional grant was the device that assumed central importance in federal-provincial accommodation, reflecting the willingness of governments merely to allocate resources and allow their activities to expand in an incremental, uncoordinated fashion. The conditional grant was an expedient instrument for financing federal-provincial initiatives, since by its nature it encourages piecemeal planning and implementation in situations where each joint venture is worked out separately from each other, from broader federal-provincial objectives and from the division of tax sources and public revenues between the two levels of government. As a result, responsibility for devising and implementing programs fell mainly to federal and provincial technicians in the appropriate program agencies.

Relatively autonomous communities of officials that cut across jurisdictional lines found that they could agree and collaborate effectively (Smiley, 1970, p. 89). In addition, the public servants were able to insulate themselves from cabinet, treasury and partisan interference. Thus, most of the important joint policy-making decisions were the product of "close and continuous collaboration between federal and provincial officials with a common professional background" (ibid., p. 62). It can safely be assumed that this situation was as favourable an environment of clientele relationships between agencies and their constituent groups as that which existed at each individual level of government. With the degree of cooperation between department officials that existed, it would be difficult to separate the two policy-making arenas. Cooperative federalism could be collaborative or collusive federalism.

The changes in the nature of the state and in the policy-making structures within the intergovernmental arena during the late 1960s and 1970s described by Simeon and Schultz reflect the general changes in the Canadian political system. When the politicians became aware that federal-provincial relations were central to achieving their broader policy objectives, they were no longer willing to leave the setting of policy details to their program technicians to work out. Therefore, responsibility for federal-provincial relations was partially taken away from line departments and placed in the hands of cabinet and its central agencies at both levels of government. The economic interdependence of governments made it necessary that they not only coordinate their own internal operations but also their actions with each other, so as not to frustrate each other's policy initiatives.

While Parliament, pressure groups and the general public suffer because of the undue secrecy of first ministers' conferences, this is certainly no less true of cabinet deliberations. The system as a whole has become more insular, and the power vacuum created by the shift toward a planning-oriented state can create special problems for interest groups in the intergovernmental arena. As Schultz's study shows, the need of both levels of government to acquire political legitimacy for their policy initiatives can cause groups that try to participate directly in the intergovernmental process to get caught in a struggle between governments actively attempting to change the balance of power. This seriously undermines the ability of groups to perform as independent actors, since they are immediately associated and identified with the political strength of one level of government or another.

The financial restraint now practised by all governments may have unforeseen effects on the recruitment of interest groups into the intergovernmental process. On the one hand, the reduction in government expansion means that intergovernmental conflicts over responsibility for new policy areas is less likely to occur. On the other hand, financial restraint is likely to increase the tensions between levels of government, as each tries to pass its financial burdens on to the other. Interest groups can provide a "cheap" political resource at a time when financial means are scarce. The ad hoc nature of the intergovernmental process further complicates the situation to which interest groups have had to adjust themselves. There are signs that some groups are learning about the new system and how to participate in it, but this has come to mean that interest groups must adopt a new set of tactics in order to gain or retain influence. Once again, circumstances in the intergovernmental arena reflect the system at large. The discrete, incremental approach favoured by established groups is not as effective as it used to be. Cases, such as that reported by Bucovetsky, where the mining industry allied with provincial governments to oppose the federal government, are often cited as a demonstration of how powerful certain business groups are. But as Gillies claims and Berry's study shows, once government has committed itself on a general strategy, the best an interest group can do is to cooperate with government in order to mitigate its impact on the group. This post facto approach has very little effect on the general policy direction of government. Groups must get to government before policy is determined, and this favours the institutionalized groups.

Issue-oriented groups on the other hand have had greater success so far by taking advantage of the increase in public debate surrounding highly politicized intergovernmental issues. The first clear example of this was the constitutional debate of 1980, in which the native spokesmen and the women's lobby were both able to ensure that their rights were recognized in the new Canadian Constitution. However, one must recall that this followed the courts' reprimand to the federal government, requiring it to obtain substantial agreement. To mobilize support it felt compelled to open up the process to groups using the parliamentary committee hearings.

Douglas Sanders' account of the native groups' lobbying activities reveals a skilful use of the media in order to exert moral suasion on the federal government. The Indians' opposition to the Charter was particularly troubling because it combined moral and legal argument. "The government knew that the Indian cause had significant appeal in Canada, as well as in Britain" (Sanders, 1983, p. 314). The Indians' visits to Britain were well covered by the Canadian media. The federal government was forced again and again to make concessions because of the political embarrassment being caused to Canada's image abroad plus the fear that the British Parliament might be convinced by the Indians' representatives. When aboriginal rights were dropped from the Charter in the "November Accord," the previous public attention given to the issue allowed the Indians to go public and embarrass the federal and provincial governments into reinserting Section 34. However, it was the Joint Senate-Commons Committee on the Constitution, established by the federal government as a means of building a broader federal consensus, that provided the central vehicle for serious involvement in the policy-making process and for sustained political as well as public attention.

Hosek's study of the women's lobby shows that it received less media attention than had the native lobby, but when equality rights for women were dropped from the Charter in order to secure provincial support for the "November Accord," they too were able to embarrass governments into reinstating them. All along, the federal government has sought civil rights groups' support by claiming that it was the only level of government interested in protecting civil rights. Public attention was ultimately effective against the provinces as well:

> . . . the lobbying of the provinces served to reveal the political vulnerability of provincial governments on human rights issues, especially when they are not protected by the intergovernmental process. When first ministers negotiate as a group, no single one of them can be held responsible for the decision reached. The lobbying of women's groups shone a spotlight on each premier individually, and in that context no premier dared to refuse, as a matter of principle, to entrench equality for women in the constitution of Canada.
>
> (Hosek, 1983, p. 293)

In both these cases, it was obvious that the interest group had to take advantage of every possible opportunity and every weakness in order to achieve its goals.

Another important forum for the participation of interest groups in the intergovernmental process was provided by the Parliamentary Task Force on Fiscal Federalism (the Breau Task Force). This task force did its work before the federal governmental prepared its bargaining position on fiscal relations with the provinces. Simeon and Dunn suggest that it is possible that:

> . . . the federal government saw that, given the model of the constitutional committee, the Task Force might generate public support for the greater visibility and presence Ottawa was now seeking.
>
> (Simeon and Dunn, 1982, p. 110)

A large majority of the groups that participated were social welfare and health groups, plus a few labour groups; there were almost none from business. Group involvement in the task force provided functional input into the governmental process. The task force found that "virtually all groups felt Ottawa should be more than a transfer mechanism" (ibid., p. 115). Yet, they were not entirely pro-centralist. Their major concern was that adequate social and health services be provided to all Canadians, and most felt that this should involve a cooperative effort by both levels of government:

> The general approach, then, was to look to the federal government for assistance by ensuring it maintained its funding, and used those funds to require provinces to serve the groups' desired objectives. Pressure on Ottawa was seen as a way of bringing pressure on the provinces. Most groups appeared to believe that it was somehow safer to be clients of only one level of government.
>
> (ibid., p. 119)

Simeon and Dunn conclude that the parliamentary task force, as with the constitutional experience, provided an arena for those excluded from the intergovernmental process itself and allowed the range and definition of problems to be broadened. These examples indicate that the increased public scrutiny that has resulted from government secrecy has made it at times more difficult for governments to define the public interest in the way they see fit. As Hosek observes about the charter debate, "the demand for wider public participation in the process of constitutional change was to become far stronger than Ottawa had expected" (Hosek, 1983, p. 286). Participation in these issues has also educated groups as to their interests in the intergovernmental process and how it operates.

There are, however, serious flaws concerning the effectiveness of this form of participation. The dependence on media coverage and public opinion is a fragile means of influencing government. The loss of either can result in government turning a deaf ear. Issue-oriented groups have little choice in the matter, since their capacity to carry on sustained negotiations with government is very limited. Sanders' analysis reveals the difficulty that the native groups had in their actual dealings with government, because they were so politically unsophisticated and divided. Therefore, negotiation was never a real possibility "since a truly accommodative response from government would have exposed the political weakness of the organization" (Sanders, 1983, p. 324). Institutionalized groups are in an equally awkward position, for while they have the capacity to conduct sustained consultation with government, to adopt the public methods that have been effective in intergovernmental issues would also alienate them from the agencies with which they have close connections.

Another serious limitation for interest groups, which becomes obvious from these studies, is that the initiative to provide them with access often stems from the government itself:

> . . . American women had to struggle for years to put equal rights on the political agenda, and it was not at all clear that Canadian women would have been any more successful on their own had the government not announced the idea of a Charter . . . the terms of the Canadian debate and the timetable for its resolution were set by governments, and women were able to manoeuvre only within the narrow spaces afforded them by elected political leaders.
>
> (Hosek, 1983, p. 283)

While government cannot always ignore the opinions that it has itself surveyed, it reserves the right to determine what it will adopt and what not. The federal government was quick to draw on the Breau Task Force as evidence that a national consensus existed for the protection of national standards in health care. However, its recommendation that federal funding for the medicare program be maintained was ignored, and funds to the provinces cut back. The financial dependence on the federal government of many of these small groups who are participating lends support to the claim that their involvement is closely monitored by Ottawa.

Will the federal government continue to canvass interest group opinion? The kinds of demands that groups make will be an important factor. Insofar as they define their interests in relation to the balance of powers between levels of government, they will be a resource for whichever side is favoured and seeks to exploit its opportunity. But to the extent that groups make purely functional as opposed to national-regional demands on governments (for example, equal pay for work of equal value as opposed to greater federal responsibility over family law), their affiliation will be less politically advantageous. Simeon observes with respect to the Breau Task Force:

> The clear lesson of these interventions was that the substantive interests of groups were strongly affected by the intergovernmental relationship but that groups had little direct access to the process. Several groups proposed creation of tripartite — federal-provincial, and sectoral — councils in which both governments and affected interests would come together to evaluate policy and make recommendations. (Simeon, 1982, p. 50)

Clearly, the development of formalized mechanisms for interest group involvement in intergovernmental relations would be a considerable advance over the present situation. Despite this pessimistic assessment, attempts have been made to develop mechanisms for pressure group involvement.

Mechanisms for Pressure Group Involvement in Intergovernmental Relations

These mechanisms can be roughly divided into formal and informal. Formal mechanisms offer well-defined involvement with some sort of legal or administrative status. Informal mechanisms are irregular, spontaneous and ill-defined involvement often based on networks of personal contacts. Formal mechanisms include such devices as advisory councils and deputations to appear before committees of Parliament or cabinet. Informal mechanisms include the various forms of lobbying, public protests and public relations. As indicated above, reliance on informal mechanisms for participating in intergovernmental relations leads to questionable results. Both institutionalized and issue-oriented groups have difficulty determining and rationalizing the place of interest groups in a process where provincial governments make legitimate demands for greater provincial autonomy and control over their spending and the federal government seeks to establish itself as the legitimate voice of the national interest.

There are two kinds of formalized mechanisms that have been developed so far: those that allow interest groups to participate at one level of government or another and those that involve joint discussions between federal and provincial governments and interest groups. Formal mechanisms of the first sort have recently been widely reported. The Joint Senate-Commons Committee on the Constitution allowed groups the opportunity to express their views on the Constitution independently of government, and the result was a major shift in the terms of the debate. The emphasis placed on the government-citizen relationship challenged the monopoly and legitimacy of the federal-provincial process as the only means of structuring issues.

The Breau Task Force, established on the initiative of the federal opposition (especially the NDP), was another instrument for bringing together governments and groups in a single body to discuss federal-provincial issues. Both of these mechanisms provided the additional benefit of an early access by Parliament to the negotiation of federal-provincial issues. "The [Breau Task Force's] first recommendation was that, prior to future intergovernmental negotiations on fiscal arrangements, Parliament again have a similar opportunity for consultation with the public" (Simeon and Dunn, 1982, p. 119).

While these mechanisms alleviate some of the difficulties involved with infiltrating the intergovernmental process itself, there are drawbacks. Because they are not a permanent part of the policy-making process, groups are still dependent on government to determine to which debates they will be allowed formally to contribute. Nor is government compelled to follow their advice, unless public support is overwhelmingly in the group's favour. In fact, the groups are often put in the position where they must react to government initiatives. They are in danger of being manipulated by the new *dirigiste* state. Certainly they are the weaker partner and generally have to give better than they get. They can only respond when government provides an opportunity, so they are usually really accomplices rather than countervailing forces in the policy-making process.

There is reason to believe that the trend toward ad hoc interest group consultation is being used as a means of legitimizing actions which require the cooperation of the other level of government. This was particularly true of the Liberal federal government (1984), whose ability to act in the name of the national interest was hindered by the fact that its electoral representation was not representative of the country. Audrey Doerr's research on the role of coloured papers shows that the number of policy papers released by the federal government has increased dramatically over the past twenty years and that the vast majority "either touch on provincial jurisdiction or are in areas in which the federal government requires provincial cooperation" (Doerr, 1982, p. 374). The task force mechanism seems to provide another means of harnessing interest group support in order to neutralize provincial opposition to federal initiatives.

The literature also reveals a second model for interest group involvement in intergovernmental issues that is perhaps more prevalent than is generally thought. Forums for interaction of interest group representatives with representatives of both levels of government exist in a wide variety of areas.

In 1969 Gérard Veilleux surveyed the machinery for intergovernmental cooperation (Veilleux, 1979). The bulk of this machinery involved only two levels of government. However, he notes that representatives of interest groups, as well as other individuals, participate in important joint forums. For example, the Dominion Council of Health, established in 1919, met twice a year to act as an advisory committee to the minister of National Health and Welfare. It is composed of the federal deputy minister, provincial deputy ministers and representatives of agricultural, labour, rural and women's organizations. More recently (1962), the National Council of Welfare was established. Like the Dominion Council of Health, it is composed of the relevant deputy ministers and regional private welfare and associated interest groups.

Veilleux cites other examples of joint forums in the area of agriculture and tourism. R.M. Burns described in 1976 the Conference of Mines Ministers as a joint intergovernmental interest group forum which "is considered a suitable occasion for discrete lobbying." The 1973 meeting, Burns reported, involved federal-provincial and industry representation on a variety of technical committees.

Perhaps the most ambitious attempt at establishing genuine interest group involvement in the federal-provincial process is the extensive series of tripartite discussions involving business, labour and federal and provincial representatives that were held in 1978 (called Tier I and Tier II) to facilitate the formulation of a national economic strategy. Two policy-making sessions were conducted concurrently. In one (the Federal-Provincial Conference on the Economy), the provinces and the federal government discussed in detail the formulation of a medium-term economic strategy. It included a large number of ministerial meetings and two large-scale summit conferences of first ministers. In the other, the federal Ministry of Industry, Trade and Commerce arranged a series of meetings with business, labour and provincial governments to deal with industrial development in a large number of sectors. Some of the participants from the business and labour communities were suspicious of this government initiative, questioning whether their opinions would be taken seriously:

> But many people in the private sector believed that the federal government's approach to consultation was changing. Like some provincial officials, they thought that Ottawa, having found itself in a policy vacuum, was beginning to seek genuine input from the other economic forces.
>
> (Brown and Eastman, 1981, p. 122)

A serious flaw that hindered the success of this experiment was that the government-group task forces were not geared specifically to what each sector could contribute to the larger, macroeconomic goals. Instead, they became forums for special pleading, with labour and management in each sector presenting government with suggestions for concessions and assistance to help them in their businesses. This provided the government with little insight as to how the overall Canadian economy could best be led to recovery.

Douglas Brown and Julia Eastman conclude that if the public and private sectors are to overcome their respective ignorance of each other, then consultation with the private sector must move beyond its present ad hoc status. Noting the inherent tension between a policy-making process based on federal-provincial negotiation and one based on functional concerns, they propose that industry consultative forums might be more successful if they were tied to the federal process at a less political level. They proposed such instruments as joint planning agencies.

It should be noted that such mechanisms seem to have functioned almost exclusively as a means of consultation at the bureaucratic level. They do not exhibit the characteristics for joint decision-making that would allow them to be described as corporatist. Indeed, Brown and Eastman note that the sectoral as well as regional fragmentation of interest groups representing business and labour did present a barrier to their effective participation in the Tier I and Tier II consultative process.

Governments have resisted interest group efforts to become more involved in intergovernmental negotiations. If they were formally introduced into the process, they could seriously challenge it by rejecting accommodations reached by governments. Nevertheless, it is by no means clear that all groups would welcome the opportunity to participate in such decision making, since it carries the risk for interest groups that their objectives might be downplayed in the process of reaching compromise. They would be within their rights to decline to participate.

In sum, there seems to be a need to formalize the role of interest groups in the policy-making process in order to restore their ability to act as informed and independent agents. With government involvement, both federal and provincial, in the complexities of everyday life, the groups that this process has called into being have an essential role to play in the process of decision making. Only they can supply some of the information and the experience that are essential to policy making. They, therefore, have a legitimacy today which is much greater than was the case before governments became so intimately involved in the complexities of our modern society. This is especially true of the groups that speak for the established capitalist interests in society. Their collaboration is essential to government. Yet, no modern popularly elected government can be seen to rely too heavily upon such rich and powerful interests, so place has to be made at the table for the issue-oriented groups with a more popular base.

Governments (both federal and provincial), therefore, are engaged in an ongoing bargaining process with both the established institutionalized groups and the more ephemeral popular groups speaking for mass opinion, often on single issues. There are, therefore, two continuous processes going on: relations between governments (especially federal and provincial, but also inter-provincial and provincial-municipal), and group government relations at both the federal and provincial levels.

The separation of the federal-provincial process from the government group interaction is surely most unfortunate, because important components to any sound policy decision must take into account both perspectives and the point of view of all three orders of players: the interest groups, the provincial governments and the federal government.

Chapter 5

Interest Group Perceptions of Government and the Intergovernmental Process

Since the modern welfare state has been led to intervene so deeply in the lives of the people and in the economic life of the country, it has aroused great expectations of security for all from every part of the community. Groups are made aware of the susceptibility of government to pressure, and this mobilizes them in a competitive scramble for the support of government. Groups are organized to defend their various interests, and an array of single interest groups now confronts the state. This is amply demonstrated by comparing the submissions to the three royal commissions on the overall functioning of Canada's economy: the Royal Commission on Dominion-Provincial Relations, established in 1937 (the Rowell-Sirois Commission), the Royal Commission on Canada's Economic Prospects (the Gordon Commission, 1957), and the Royal Commission on the Economic Union and Development Prospects for Canada (the Macdonald Commission), established in 1982.

While it is always somewhat hazardous to compare submissions to one commission with those of another in a different period of time, the differences in this case are so great that some generalizations seem warranted. In the case of the two earlier commissions, reflecting the conditions of the 1930s and the 1950s, the number of briefs submitted is roughly similar, although the differences between one classification and another are at times great. However, the overall impression one has is of an interest group structure in the country which appears fairly constant. On the other hand, there were almost two and one-half times more submissions to the Macdonald Commission, reflecting the changed conditions of the 1980s. Also, there are many new types of groups participating. Some of these did not submit briefs in the earlier periods; others did not even exist.

**Submissions to Three Royal Commissions on the Canadian Economy
1937, 1957, 1982**

	Rowell-Sirois 1937	Gordon 1957	Macdonald 1982[a]
Labour	2	17	61
Business associations & private companies	67	202	254
Professional associations	26	10	43
Federal government	24	3	34
Provincial & territorial governments	118	20	40
Municipal & regional organizations	45	23	67
Native people's groups	0	0	27
Women's organizations	4	1	34
Religious agencies	4	1	12
Social service & health groups	5	1	37
Political parties	3	1	12
Seniors organizations	0	1	6
Educational & research institutions	4	11	36
Voluntary & special interest	29	6	234
	331	297	897

a. Figures not final at time of research.

This increased mobilization of interest groups, legitimized by the belief in pluralist democracy, has created a vastly expanded demand for consultation with government. This in turn makes it even more difficult for government to take its distance and elaborate overarching plans for the overall national well-being.

This chapter attempts to show Canadian interest group attitudes relating to a variety of key issues, such as government intervention in the economy, federal-provincial relations, and questions of the Canadian economic union. The means by which this will be attempted is an examination of the briefs presented to the Macdonald Commission.

The Briefs to the Commission

To explain the methodology employed, as well as to appreciate its limitations, it is necessary to understand how the Commission dealt with and catalogued the briefs. (The word *brief* includes not only the submissions to the Commission but also the transcripts of presentations made by numerous organizations to the Commission as it travelled across the country in 1983.)

In order to cope with the substantial volume of submissions (40,000 pages of briefs and 15,831 pages of transcripts), the staff of the Commission first created a subject classification for the briefs. This simple classification had to be elaborated in order to permit an analysis of the content of the briefs; therefore a content analysis methodology was constructed. Every text (brief or transcript) was read and the main ideas extracted; then the data were classified by topic. It was hoped that this would minimize the inevitable subjectivity involved in the analysis.

The topics were divided into seven major categories, which in turn were subdivided into 52 subject areas; these were further subdivided into 300 topics. These were the bases for classifying the quotations and brief summaries which formed the material for our analysis.

In addition to classifying the subject matter of the briefs, the staff of the Commission also classified into broad categories the organizations that submitted briefs or made representations. Three of these — industry and commerce (generally noted as "business"), labour and voluntary associations — were examined for this study. The other broad categories created by the Commission included governments and their agencies and educational organizations. A large number of briefs were also submitted by individuals.

Each of the organizations was classified by province. In addition, the industry and commerce interest groups were classified by the Commission according to the sectoral nature of their activities, such as agriculture, forest products, transportation, manufacturing and financial institutions.

The labour organizations were classified according to the federation with which each was affiliated. Included in the "voluntary" sector were very divergent types of organizations. Among these were: women's groups, arts and culture, health/social services, native peoples' groups, religious agencies, groups representing seniors, youth organizations and multicultural groups.

Methodology

The analysis is limited to three sectors of interest groups: business, labour and voluntary. Voluntary associations are included in the analysis primarily for the purpose of comparison with the business and labour organizations. The excerpts from the briefs and transcripts in the categories that appeared relevant were scanned. From this preliminary examination were selected the briefs which specifically addressed at least one of the issues chosen for analysis.

For each issue under investigation, a range of possible positions was determined. All groups which addressed the issue were classified according to one of these options.

The positions have been broken down according to "region" for all three categories of groups that are examined (business, labour and voluntary). These permitted a determination of any link between a group's position on a particular issue and the area of the country where it is situated.

Furthermore, where it was possible, the "business" groups were divided according to primary, manufacturing and service sectors. This was accomplished by grouping the business organizations according to the classification system which the Commission had used. Those groups which were in one of the following categories were deemed to be "primary" sector organizations: natural resources, oil and gas companies, forest products, mining industries, fishing industry and agriculture. Those which fell into one of the following categories were considered to be "secondary" sector groups: manufacturing industries, transportation and communications. Lastly, financial institutions, consulting firms and law firms were classifed as "tertiary" sector groups.

The system used by the Commission had a separate category for "trade associations"; all such organizations were grouped together, regardless of the sector they represented. In undertaking the sectoral analysis of the business briefs, it seemed sensible to include, where possible, the "trade association" briefs with the briefs from the particular sectors they represented. Still, it was not possible to fit all of the business briefs into one or other of these categories. For example, chambers of commerce and some of the trade associations represent a wide spectrum of businesses, so it was not possible to place these into one particular sector. Hence, these organizations were put into a separate "omnibus" category.

Limitations of the Methodology

Perhaps the most important methodological limitation relates to the arbitrariness involved in reducing a brief, often containing complex economic argumentation, to short statements. This, however, is necessary in order to make any sort of comparison. Of course, such an approach limits the strength of the conclusions, which necessarily must be of a "more or less" nature. Moreover, an analysis that focusses on the number of groups addressing a particular issue does not take into account the relative importance of these groups in society. *Who* says something is often more important than *how many* adopt one position as opposed to another. Any statistical analysis of the briefs must be treated cautiously.

The analysis is of course limited to those organizations that actually submitted briefs or made presentations to the Commission. This seriously qualifies any generalizations about Canadian interest groups, based on the findings. This is especially true given the paucity of briefs from some of the major segments of the Canadian economy, notably, the multinational corporations.

Another difficulty relates to the classification system used by the Commission. Although the Commission has created 300 subjects into which the briefs and transcripts are divided, none corresponds exactly to the issues being addressed in this analysis. For example, the Commission has a category entitled "foreign investment." While this is of central interest, the specific concern here is with the extent to which foreign investment is perceived as detrimental or beneficial to the Canadian economy. Some of the excerpts that have been included in the "foreign investment" classification do not address this specific issue and, hence, were not included in the analysis. Moreover, excerpts in several of the Commission's categories often address the same issue. Some organizations are represented with respect to the same issue in more than one category. Where this has occurred, each organization is treated only once in the analysis. With the creation of these classifications, though, an additional element of subjectivity is introduced into the methodology.

The conclusions relating to the regional breakdown of responses on any issue must be qualified. First, each organization has been classified according to an individual province. The Commission has made no allowance for associations that are national federations comprised of provincial or regional bodies. Clearly, the interests of these groups are national in scope, extending beyond the boundaries of the province where their head offices are located.

Second, it is acknowledged that some business associations and some individual corporations in Canada are more "regional" than others. These often represent industries that are not national in scope. Other industries and companies do not exist in one region only but are active in several or all regions of the country.

The Issues

The study focusses on three general areas of interest: first, perceptions of government, primarily with respect to intervention in the economy; second, perceptions of the intergovernmental process and the locus of decision making; and third, impressions about the economic union and regionalism.

Within each of these areas, three or four specific issues are examined. Following is the framework for the analysis:

1. Perceptions of Government:
   Government Intervention in the Economy
   Industrial Strategy
   Foreign Investment and Ownership
   Consultation between Government and Interest Groups

2. Perceptions of Federal-Provincial Relations:
   Nature of Federal-Provincial Relations
   Division of Powers
   Decentralization

3. The Economic Union and Regionalism:
   The Economic Union
   Regional Development Policy
   Senate Reform

In all, the perceptions of interest groups on ten specific issues are examined. In the analysis of each of these, the focus is on the importance of the particular issue to the various interest groups in Canada. Since the briefs presented to the Commission touch upon myriad issues, the question here is: how many and which groups considered these specific issues important enough to address?

The concern is not simply with which groups address these issues. Rather, it is to determine the actual positions held with respect to each of the issues being studied. Which groups hold similar positions and which are at opposite ends of a spectrum? What evidence is there of cleavages that form, first, along regional lines, and second, along sectoral or other lines?

In addition to analyzing the perceptions of various interest groups, we consider the question of how these compare with the opinions of the federal and provincial governments and agencies. Unfortunately, the number of presentations from governments is not large, as few federal departments or agencies submitted briefs. Perhaps the best source of federal opinion is the presentations made by several of the Liberal cabinet ministers. There are clearly limitations to using this small sample of briefs to represent the position of the federal government, despite the rule of cabinet solidarity. Nevertheless, the comments made by the federal representatives in areas relevant to the analysis provide evidence of whether there is any congruence of perception with those in the business, labour and voluntary sectors.

Several of the provincial governments submitted briefs or made presentations to the Commission. These positions were scrutinized to determine how the perceptions of provincial governments compared with those of the interest groups.[1]

Perceptions of Government

The analysis of the briefs to determine the interest group perceptions of government focusses on four areas: attitudes toward government intervention in the economy, an "industrial strategy," the level of foreign investment and ownership in the economy, and the amount of consultation between government and society.

GOVERNMENT INTERVENTION IN THE ECONOMY

The briefs that directly address the question of government intervention were grouped in three clusters along a continuum.

A word of caution must be injected here. As the task is to compare the positions of all groups addressing a particular issue, it is necessary to define categories in a rather broad and amorphous fashion. The purpose is to determine which groups hold essentially the same view on a particular issue, even though these views may be expressed in a variety of ways. The three categories of positions relating to government intervention in the economy represent groupings around three distinct points on a continuum.

The first is a pro–free-market stance, which advocates a reduction in the size of government and/or the extent of its involvement in the economy. This position emphasizes the role of the private sector, with government relegated primarily to the role of "facilitator."

The second, more intermediate, position advocates a strong role for the private sector but acknowledges a function for government beyond that of mere facilitator (for example, as protector of minorities).

The third position is essentially the antithesis of the first. It underlines the need for substantial government involvement in the economy — either generally, or in a specific policy area. The emphasis made in a brief is important in assigning it to a particular category. If, for example, a brief emphasizes the need for a limited government role, it is classified under the first option. If, however, the focus is on the need for a government role in the economy, it is placed in the third category.

	Business	Labour	Voluntary
Option 1	53	0	8
Option 2	21	6	14
Option 3	11	8	3

An overwhelming proportion of the business groups endorse the first position, whereas all of the labour groups adopt either the second or the third options. The positions of the voluntary sector are distributed among all three. The implication here is that labour, and to some extent the voluntary sector, is more likely to prefer an interventionist role for government than are business groups.

The majority of business sector briefs argue in general terms against increased government involvement in the economy. Following are three examples of the "facilitative" role that business generally prescribes for government:

[The B.C. Mining Industry Association suggests that] Canadian economic performance over the long term would be strengthened if governments would pursue facilitative rather than interventionist policies — that is, policies that support the private sector's efforts to expand the economy's natural areas of strength, rather than policies that create or maintain industries artificially in the face of adverse economic signals. The benefits of trade are too significant to be sacrificed so casually.

(*Mining Association of British Columbia*, Brief, August 23, 1983, p.10)

Governments have a crucial role to play in economic development. Government must decide the direction the economy is to take, and then work with industry to permit it to achieve the desired goals. Government must create the environment to which entrepreneurs are attracted and in which they will flourish. (*H.N. Halvorson*, Brief, August 19, 1983, p. 4)

Government's role is to be responsible for the legislative and regulatory environment which would be compatible with a revival of business sector initiative. (*Burns Fry Ltd.*, Brief, November 24, 1983, p. 2)

Some of the voluntary organizations support this view toward government intervention as well: two argue for decreased government intervention and greater support for voluntary action. "No citizen of Canada should expect government to do everything for him!" (*United Way of Thompson*, Brief, October 7, 1983, p. 1)

Some of the business groups, as well as several from the labour and voluntary sectors, do support the third option. A few of these adopt a general interventionist stance, arguing for a significant role for government in the economy. Typical of these is the brief from the *Labour Council of Metropolitan Toronto*, which asserts that government plays a critical role "in generating economic prosperity" (Brief, November 1, 1983, p. 7). The *B.C. Association of Social Workers* argues for increased public initiatives in order to stimulate private investment. Many of the briefs in this third category support the notion of an "industrial strategy." (See the following section.)

Business Sector

	Primary	Secondary	Tertiary	Omnibus[a]
Option 1	11	11	13	18
Option 2	6	6	2	7
Option 3	4	1	2	4

a. Includes chambers of commerce and other associations that do not represent a single sector of the economy, as well as professional associations and other groups that do not easily fit into the primary, secondary and tertiary categories. Within the business community, while most seem to support a "facilitative" role for government, there are some groups in each of the primary, secondary and service sectors which are classified in the second and third categories.

Some of the organizations advocate significant roles for government in their own particular sectors of the economy. These include appeals for more government involvement in the agricultural sector, land use policy and the meat industry. There is one brief expressing opposition to deregulation in the airline industry.

Another aspect of government involvement in the economy relates to "affirmative action"-type programs. *Le Réseau d'action et d'information pour les femmes* argues for a government role in helping to create an equal situation for women in the economy (Brief, November 1, 1983,

p. 35). *La fédération des franco-colombiens* asserts that governments ought to weigh the impact of their policies on the francophone community (Brief, August 31, 1983, p. 8).

Region

	Atlantic	Quebec	Ontario	Prairies	B.C.	Terr.
Business						
Option 1	2	11	23	10	7	–
Option 2	4	3	9	4	1	–
Option 3	–	–	6	2	2	1
Labour						
Option 1	–	–	–	–	–	–
Option 2	–	2	2	2	–	–
Option 3	–	3	3	1	1	–
Voluntary						
Option 1	1	1	3	3	–	–
Option 2	2	3	4	2	3	–
Option 3	–	–	1	1	1	–

A regional breakdown of the results suggests that region is not a significant factor in influencing a group's position with respect to government intervention. This is somewhat surprising, given the very substantial efforts to bring about "regional economic expansion" by governments — which must have benefited business in the less developed regions.

INDUSTRIAL STRATEGY

One form of government intervention in the economy is to adopt an "industrial strategy," or long-term planning. The concept of an industrial strategy and a central planning role for the government has been debated in Canada for several years. This analysis is confined to the briefs that actually mention an industrial strategy, or long-term planning. It is useful to determine which groups found it important enough to register either their support or opposition to such a concept in their presentations to the Commission. Option 1 supports the concept of an industrial strategy, or long-term planning; whereas Option 2 registers opposition to this.

	Business	Labour	Voluntary
Option 1	7	5	6
Option 2	8	1	0

These results suggest that the business community is evenly divided on this issue. The other segments of society, however, seem clearly to favour an industrial strategy. Of the 12 briefs from the labour and voluntary sectors which speak of such a concept, only one opposes it.

Many of the business organizations tend to oppose the concept of an industrial strategy, generally, and the notion of "picking winners" in particular. For example, the *Bank of Montreal* argues:

> Placing greater reliance on market forces implies rejection of the idea of an all-encompassing "industrial policy." If greater efficiency and productivity are to be promoted in the private sector, policy must be directed toward promoting greater market discipline. Let the marketplace, not economic planners, mete out the rewards and punishments.
>
> (Brief, November 17, 1983, p. 16)

Other examples include: the *Canadian Manufacturers' Association*, which argues that "market forces will determine winners, and governments should not try to pick them" (Brief, September 6, 1983, p. 30); *Burns Fry Ltd.*, which asserts that: "New directions in industrial development must come from the business sector itself" (Brief, November 24, 1983, p. 1); and the *Mining Association of British Columbia*: "The pursuit of an industrial policy . . . is almost certainly a snare and a delusion" (Brief, August 23, 1983, p. 8).

Examples of the opposite position include: the *SNC Group*, which supports backing winners and *Nordicity Group*, which states in its presentation to the Commission:

> . . . we need to set in place and sustain a long term industrial policy which aims at capturing new industrial, particularly high technology, opportunities and which focuses on import replacement and develops goods and services related to social priorities that are emerging, for example, those that are related to an aging society.
>
> (Roger Voyer, *Nordicity Group Ltd.*, Transcript, Ottawa, December 15, 1983 [vol.73], p.15336)

The *Association of Professional Engineers of Saskatchewan* calls for a "made in Canada Industrial Strategy [to] to be based on our strengths synchronized to the world's needs" (Brief, November 1, 1983, p. 3); and the *Calgary Council for Advanced Technology* argues that a "national industrial strategy is needed, because many difficult choices will have to be made" (Brief, October 25, 1983, p. 5).

Region

	Atlantic	Quebec	Ontario	Prairies	B.C.	Terr.
Business						
Option 1	2	1	1	2	1	–
Option 2	–	2	4	–	2	–
Labour						
Option 1	1	1	1	1	1	–
Option 2	1	–	–	–	–	–
Voluntary						
Option 1	1	–	4	1	–	–
Option 2	–	–	–	–	–	–

A regional breakdown suggests that there is some support for such a strategy in all regions of the country. All of the opposition, however, is from Central Canada and British Columbia.

Business Sector

	Primary	Secondary	Tertiary	Omnibus
Option 1	–	1	2	4
Option 2	1	2	3	2

A breakdown of the business briefs by sector seems to suggest that the issue of an industrial strategy is not a concern for the resource-based industries. Although the numbers here are very small, there is evidence that both a regional cleavage and the basic business-labour cleavage divide interest groups on the issue of an industrial strategy.

FOREIGN INVESTMENT AND OWNERSHIP

One specific aspect of government involvement in the economy concerns policies directed at the level of foreign investment and foreign control of the Canadian economy. The Foreign Investment Review Agency (FIRA) has been under fire from various parts of the business community since its inception. This analysis of the briefs to the Commission seeks to ascertain the interests that oppose those policies of the Canadian government intended to curb the level of foreign investment in this country.

Four general positions are posited. The first supports foreign capital in Canada, often arguing that it is necessary for the Canadian economy to grow. Federal government policies that curb the inflow of capital are said to hurt the Canadian economy and society. The second position attacks FIRA itself, castigating it primarily for its slowness and inconsistency in application.

The third position is an intermediate one, acknowledging some value in the government's promotion of Canadianization, but asserting that foreign investment remains important to Canada. The fourth and final category supports the goals of FIRA and/or opposes the level of foreign control in Canada (Option 4).

	Business	Labour	Voluntary
Option 1	21	–	–
Option 2	11	–	–
Option 3	2	–	–
Option 4	7	5	3

There is substantial opposition from the business community to policies that limit foreign investment, as well as support for allowing foreign capital into Canada. An example of the general business stance comes from this presentation by the *Saskatchewan Chamber of Commerce*, which argues that foreign investment:

> . . . has contributed significantly to the development of this country and should be given a greater and more important supportive environment. Thus, Canadianization policies, such as the experience with the National Energy Program, in our view, should not have been developed in the first place and should definitely not be extended.
>
> (Transcript, Regina, November 24, 1983 [vol. 51], p. 10655)

On the other side, two business bodies, *SNC Group* and *Machinery and Equipment Manufacturers Association of Canada* register their support for Canadian content requirements. The *Canadian Shipbuilding and Ship Repairing Association* points out that most foreign shipbuilders are heavily subsidized by their respective national governments.

Business Sector

	Primary	Secondary	Tertiary	Omnibus
Option 1	3	6	4	8
Option 2	1	5	3	2
Option 3	–	–	1	1
Option 4	2	2	3	0

A sectoral analysis of the briefs from the business community reveals that within all three sectors, there is more support than opposition for foreign investment in Canada. There is, however, a small amount of opposition (Option 4) within all of the business sectors.

The stance of the business community contrasts sharply with the opinions of the labour and the voluntary sectors. Not many groups in these latter two sectors comment on this issue; of those who do, however, all adopt the fourth option, condemning the level of foreign ownership in the Canadian economy.

For example, the *B.C. and Yukon Territory Building Trade Council* asserts that "the underlying problems afflicting the Canadian economy are foreign ownership and control of major industries" (Transcript, Vancouver, September 7, 1983 [vol. 2], p. 360). The *Community Forum on Shared Responsibility* concludes: "Foreign investment means that even profitable Canadian plants can be closed" (Brief, November 3, 1983, p. 1).

Region

	Atlantic	Quebec	Ontario	Prairies	B.C.	Terr.
Business						
Option 1	–	3	12	4	1	1
Option 2	1	–	8	–	1	1
Option 3	–	–	2	–	–	–
Option 4	–	3	3	1	–	–
Labour						
Option 1	–	–	–	–	–	–
Option 2	–	–	–	–	–	–
Option 3	–	–	–	–	–	–
Option 4	–	1	2	1	1	–
Voluntary						
Option 1	–	–	–	–	–	–
Option 2	–	–	–	–	–	–
Option 3	–	–	–	–	–	–
Option 4	–	–	3	–	–	–

A breakdown by region suggests that this issue is of much greater concern to groups in Central Canada than in the other regions. Of the 49 briefs that address the issue of foreign investment and control, 37 are from Quebec and Ontario.

CONSULTATION

A fourth perception of the business, labour and voluntary sectors concerns consultation between governments and interest groups. A large number of groups mentioned in their briefs to the Commission the need for more consultation and/or more effective input into the government decision-making processes. No group took the opposite position with regard to consultation. Therefore, there are no significant differences among the groups that addressed this issue. What is worth determining here is which groups make this appeal for increased and more effective consultation. As well, some suggestions to facilitate this goal can be examined.

Business	Labour	Voluntary
45	12	15

The examination of the briefs that deal with consultation between the government and groups suggests that it is not strongly correlated with any of the independent variables being considered. Increased and/or improved consultation is requested by groups from most regions, representing a wide variety of sectors within society.

Region

	Atlantic	Quebec	Ontario	Prairies	B.C.	Terr.
Business	2	7	25	4	6	1
Labour	2	2	5	3	–	–
Voluntary	–	2	4	4	5	–

Business Sector

Primary	Secondary	Tertiary
10	8	9

In the demands for increased consultation, two themes tend to recur. First, there are several calls for "expert" opinion to be given an opportunity to provide input into the policy-making process. Second, there are repeated appeals for this process to be more open and less secretive.

Cadillac Fairview offers an interesting perspective. While nearly all of the groups that mentioned consultation call upon government to increase or improve its communication with groups, *Cadillac Fairview* also suggests that business ought to make a greater effort to understand public policy and the policy process (Brief, November 14, 1983, p. 14).

Some briefs contain suggestions to improve the consultation process. The creation of permanent bodies or advisory groups composed of business, labour and government representatives is suggested by various organizations (for example, *Gulf Canada*; the *Association of Consulting Engineers*; and the *Canadian Association of Social Workers*, Transcript, Calgary, November 8, 1983 [vol. 42], p. 8503)

GOVERNMENT VIEWPOINT

Generally speaking, the federal government representatives advocate an interventionist role for government in the economy. (Former) Transport Minister Lloyd Axworthy notes that "seizing the technological advantage in any industry or economic activity requires a significant effort on the part of governments, a significant contribution of resources, initiatives and leadership" (Brief, November 25, 1983, p. 12).

In a similar vein, a brief from *Petro-Canada*, a federal Crown corporation, asserts:

> The presence of the public sector in the oil and gas industry has been beneficial to Canada and may remain necessary to ensure the orderly, timely and more complete development of our energy potential.
>
> (Transcript, Toronto, December 2, 1983 [vol. 56], p. 11835)

Alberta is the only province that directly addresses, in its brief, the issue of government intervention in the economy. It favours a role for government that can be described as facilitative.

> Governments . . . must minimize interventions which distort market incentives necessary to carry on such growth-promoting activities as work effort, occupational and geographical mobility of workers, investment and saving, innovation and entrepreneurship (Government of Alberta, p. 21). The basic role of governments in Canada should be to provide a stable environment which builds the confidence of the private sector, and therefore, allows economic benefits to be created in the most effective manner.
>
> (Government of Alberta, Brief, October 31, 1983, p. 11)

Perceptions of Federal-Provincial Relations

Of particular interest to this study is the perception that interest groups have of federal-provincial interaction, the distribution of powers between the two orders of government, and the appropriate locus of decision making on the centralist-decentralist continuum. The briefs that address federal-provincial relations, the division of powers between the two levels of government, and the issue of greater decentralization are analyzed below.

THE NATURE OF FEDERAL-PROVINCIAL RELATIONS

The first option recognizes the deteriorating relations, the increased conflict, and the need for greater cooperation between the orders of government. In addition to appealing for increased federal-provincial cooperation, two other positions are also established. One is to appeal for a clarification of jurisdictional boundaries in some specific area of policy. The other position, opposite to the first, is to express satisfaction with federal-provincial relations.

	Business	Labour	Voluntary
Option 1	21	2	5
Option 2	3	–	1
Option 3	1	–	–

Only 33 of 592 organizations made reference to federal-provincial relations. Of the 25 business, two labour and six voluntary sector briefs, all but five decry the acrimonious relations that have existed between the orders of government and/or appeal for greater cooperation. Four express a desire for clarification of jurisdictional problems in specific policy areas. Only one group (*Canadian Pulp and Paper Association*, Transcript, Thunder Bay, October 17, 1983 [vol. 26], p. 5028) expresses satisfaction with the level of cooperation between governments, and that is with respect to its own industrial sector.

Region

	Atlantic	**Quebec**	**Ontario**	**Prairies**	**B.C.**	**Terr.**
Business						
Option 1	2	3	12	3	1	–
Option 2	–	1	2	–	–	–
Option 3	–	1	–	–	–	–
Labour						
Option 1	1	–	1	–	–	–
Option 2	–	–	–	–	–	–
Option 3	–	–	–	–	–	–
Voluntary						
Option 1	–	–	5	–	–	–
Option 2	–	–	1	–	–	–
Option 3	–	–	–	–	–	–

Business Sector

	Primary	**Secondary**	**Tertiary**	**Omnibus**
Option 1	7	2	5	7
Option 2	–	2	1	–
Option 3	1	–	–	–

Which groups consider the federal-provincial process important enough to address in their presentations to the Commission? This is a question of primary significance, and a breakdown by region suggests that there is concern about relations between the two orders of government in all parts of Canada, with somewhat greater interest in Central Canada. Groups from all business sectors express the need for federal-provincial cooperation.

DIVISION OF POWERS

Concerning the briefs that specifically mention the role or jurisdiction of the federal government, the provincial, or both, a continuum with four positions was determined. At one end is a position advocating an increase in federal power or jurisdiction vis-à-vis the provincial governments (Option 1). At the opposite end is support for an increase in provincial power (Option 4). In between these poles are two positions affirming a strong federal role (Option 2) and a strong provincial role (Option 3), respectively.

	Business	Labour	Voluntary
Option 1	10	4	9
Option 2	17	–	3
Option 3	7	–	–
Option 4	1	–	–

An examination of the briefs that make specific reference to the powers of one or other of the orders of government reveals a rather significant number of organizations advocating a strong role for the federal government: ten business, four labour and six voluntary sector briefs advance positions which would actually increase the power of the federal government vis-à-vis the provinces (Option 1). Seventeen business and three voluntary sector briefs make statements that affirm the role of the federal government in some policy area (Option 2). These figures compare to seven business briefs that affirm the jurisdiction of the provinces in some realm and one brief that seems to support an increase in provincial jurisdiction.

Several of the briefs (ten) arguing for an increased federal presence at the expense of provincial jurisdiction, refer specifically to the field of education. Several organizations call for national standards and a greater role by the federal government in post-secondary education. For example, the *Canadian Association of School Administrators* asserts that the development of Canada has been hurt by the absence of a meaningful policy role in education for the federal government. Some groups argue for the creation of an Education Ministry or an Office of Education at the federal level (*Canadian Association of School Administrators*, and the *Confederation of Alberta Faculty Associations*, Transcript, Lethbridge, November 10, 1983 [vol. 44], p. 9090).

The *Association of Universities and Colleges of Canada* argues for federal-provincial cooperation in the area of post-secondary education, with the federal government having some control over how its funds are spent. *Northern Telecom Limited* acknowledges that there is a national aspect to education (Transcript, Edmonton, November 15, 1983 [vol. 46], p. 9503). *The Canadian Teachers' Federation* states:

> We are opposed to any further transfer of tax points to the provinces as a solution to their financial needs. The effect of such transfers in the past has been to diminish the power of the federal government to exercise its unique functions of revenue equalization among the provinces and its economic stabilization function in the interest of our long-term national development.
>
> (*Canadian Teachers' Federation*, Brief, November 1, 1983, p. 35)

Some of the briefs from the business community argue for an increased federal presence in other policy areas. Two business associations call for a greater interest by the federal government in the forestry sector (*Association of BC Professional Foresters*, and *Council of Forest Industries of BC* (Transcript, Vancouver, September 8, 1983 [vol. 8], p. 535). The latter, however, cautions the federal government against encroaching upon provincial jurisdiction. The *Canadian Association of Social Workers* proposes the development of concurrent powers in the area of social welfare. The *Saskatchewan Federation of Agriculture* argues that:

> . . . consideration should be given for increased Federal jurisdiction respecting stabilization programs and national marketing agencies, energy, soil and water management, export marketing, farm credit, and land use.
>
> (Brief, October 28, 1983, p. 7)

Some of the labour organizations indicate that they look mainly to the federal government for leadership. The *Ontario Public Service Employees Union* asserts that although all governments must increase their role to ensure equity and security within society, the ultimate responsibility lies with the federal government to ensure that the provinces fulfil their duties. *The National Farmers Union* recommends the creation of a national land use policy, even if it involves transferring powers from the provinces to the federal government.

Some interesting ideas, each strengthening the role of the federal government, are put forward by several of the voluntary sector associations. *The National Action Committee on the Status of Women* asserts that the federal government must continue to play an important role in providing social services to Canadian women, especially to ensure equality of services across the country. *The Lakehead Social Planning Council* argues for a federal government role in the forest resources industry despite its being a provincial responsibility. It says that Ottawa could adopt a role in this area similar to that taken with respect to social services (Transcript, Thunder Bay, October 18, 1983 [vol. 28], p. 5436).

The Status of Women Action Group states that social and welfare services should be nationally defined and not subject to radical alteration by the provincial governments. *Le réseau d'action et d'information pour les femmes* asserts that the central government should take control of the domains that are affected by interprovincial activity. *La fédération des francophones hors Québec* argues that it is the federal government's responsibility to ensure that provincial governments offer services in the French language.

Some groups do affirm the jurisdiction of the provinces. *The Canadian Federation of Independent Business* is one of the strongest advocates:

> The only way to stop the growing balkanization of the country is not to legislate against it, but to affirm the present division of powers, confirming provin-

cial jurisdiction in historic responsibilities and thus to end federal presumptions and incursions into them. (Brief, November 14, 1983, p. 3)

BP Selco Incorporated states that natural resources should continue to be owned by the provinces. Even though tax revenues derived from the resources ought to be shared between the two orders of government, the province should have the power to decide on development (Brief, December 14, 1983, p. 19).

In its brief, *Cadillac Fairview Corporation* implies that provincial powers should be increased:

It is counterproductive for the country that there is no clearer demarcation between the proper roles of the levels of government. The time appears right for a re-evaluation of the respective roles of the federal and provincial governments. A review of the division of powers, recognizing the administrative maturity and competence of the provinces, should be the next constitutional priority. (Brief, November 11, 1983, p. 19)

Region

	Atlantic	Quebec	Ontario	Prairies	B.C.	Terr.
Business						
Option 1	–	–	4	6	–	–
Option 2	4	2	9	1	1	–
Option 3	1	2	4	–	–	–
Option 4	–	–	1	–	–	–
Labour						
Option 1	1	–	1	2	–	–
Option 2	–	–	–	–	–	–
Option 3	–	–	–	–	–	–
Option 4	–	–	–	–	–	–
Voluntary						
Option 1	1	–	6	1	1	–
Option 2	–	1	1	–	1	–
Option 3	–	–	–	–	–	–
Option 4	–	–	–	–	–	–

Business Sector

	Primary	Secondary	Tertiary	Omnibus
Option 1	2	–	1	7
Option 2	3	4	1	9
Option 3	3	1	–	3
Option 4	–	–	–	1

Region does not appear to play a significant role in explaining a group's position with respect to the division of powers. An examination of only those briefs from the business community, however, suggests that the primary sector is more likely than the other sectors to favour the provincial level of government.

DECENTRALIZATION

An issue related to the division of powers is the centralization/decentralization question. To appreciate the views of the nonpolitical actors in Canadian society, we examine the briefs that address the decentralization of decision making and/or increased local autonomy. Option 1 supports greater decentralization, whereas Option 2 expresses opposition.

	Business	Labour	Voluntary
Option 1	7	2	8
Option 2	1	–	–

Region

	Atlantic	Quebec	Ontario	Prairies	B.C.	Terr.
Business						
Option 1	1	4	–	1	–	1
Option 2	1	–	–	–	–	–
Labour						
Option 1	–	2	–	–	–	–
Option 2	–	–	–	–	–	–
Voluntary						
Option 1	3	2	3	–	–	–
Option 2	–	–	–	–	–	–

Business Sector

	Primary	Secondary	Tertiary	Omnibus
Option 1	–	–	3	4
Option 2	–	–	–	1

Very few groups address the issue of decentralization. In fact, only seven business, two labour, and eight voluntary association briefs advocate decentralized decision making. Eight of the eighteen briefs originate in Quebec. All seven of the business briefs are local chambers of commerce, boards of trade, credit unions or cooperatives.

GOVERNMENT VIEWPOINT

Federal cabinet ministers refer to the need for both clarification of federal and provincial jurisdiction and for cooperation between the two levels of government. With regard to the former, Eugene Whelan, the (former) Minister of Agriculture, sees in agriculture policy a substantial amount of overlapping and duplication of services. Moreover, the overlapping of responsibilities is "an impediment to attaining rational development of the agri-food sector under the common market principle" (Brief, November 11, 1983, p. 3). The (former) Communications Minister, Francis Fox, notes that the need will arise in the future to determine the effective split of federal-provincial jurisdiction in the area of long-distance voice traffic and business services (Brief, October 31, 1983, p. 8).

The (former) Transport Minister, Lloyd Axworthy, recognizes the need for cooperation between the two orders of government:

> If the federal government is going to take a greater initiative in assisting in the development of . . . any regional economy, the making of such policy will have to be based, . . . if possible, on common agreed objectives among all levels of government, as many provincial governments are now deeply involved in policies designed to diversify their economies.
>
> (Brief, November 25, 1983, p. 17)

Four of the provincial governments appeal for increased federal-provincial cooperation, either generally or in relation to a particular policy field, such as job creation. These include: Alberta, Saskatchewan, Ontario and Nova Scotia.

Ontario also calls for a clearer division of responsibilities between the two orders of government. The Government of Alberta favours:

> limiting the use of the federal spending power in areas of provincial responsibility. . . . Alberta proposed increasing the provincial share of joint federal-provincial tax revenues, so that the provinces have access to sufficient revenues to provide the major social programs — such as health care and education — within their constitutional responsibilities.
>
> (*Government of Alberta*, Brief, October 31, 1983, p. 13)

The Economic Union and Regionalism

Of central concern to the Commission is the issue of the Canadian economic union and the rise of barriers which fragment it. The free flow of goods, capital and labour within Canada is very important to certain social groups. Policies (primarily provincial ones) that advantage one area over another are seen as detrimental to the economic union. At the federal level, however, there have been regional development policies in place that serve to promote development in specified areas of the country.

To gauge the opinion of interest groups with respect to these concerns, an examination of those groups that address the specific issues of the economic union and regional development policy is offered.

ECONOMIC UNION

No organization comes out in favour of barriers and in opposition to the concept of the economic union in Canada, or against the free mobility of labour, capital and goods. As with some of the other issues addressed, the primary concern here is to determine which groups consider the issue important enough to address. Option 1 supports the principle of the economic union and/or condemns the presence of barriers. Option 2 is a related, but separate, position: an appeal for uniformity of laws or regulations across the provinces.

	Business	Labour	Voluntary
Option 1	31	2	6
Option 2	4	0	0

As this table suggests, the issue of the economic union does not seem to be of great importance to labour and voluntary sector associations. Thirty-five business briefs address this issue.

Examples of the appeal for the preservation of the economic union and Canadian common market include:

Removal of parochial provincial barriers will encourage competition and develop efficient supplies for world markets.
(*Canadian Urban Transit Authority*, Brief, October 26, 1983, p. 8)

La création de barrières artificielles entre les provinces ne peut à long terme que nuire à l'activité agricole du pays.
(*Agrinove, coopérative agro-alimentaire*, Brief, November 3, 1983, p. 19)

We attach first priority to the enhancement of a fully integrated Canadian common market. (*Retail Council of Canada*, Brief, November 1, 1983, p. 41)

Neither do we support restraint of trade in domestic markets by the artificial application of boards or trade barriers.
(*Fisheries Council of Canada*, Brief, September 13, 1983, p. 9)

The Canadian economy needs strengthening through removal of institutional or legislative barriers to interprovincial movements of workers or goods.
(*Bell Canada Enterprises Inc.*, Brief, November 1, 1983, p. 18)

We recommend that the federal and provincial governments in Canada act at once to abolish invisible barriers to free trade and exchange between provinces. (*SNC Group*, Brief, November 28, 1983, p. 11)

Region

	Atlantic	Quebec	Ontario	Prairies	B.C.	Terr.
Business						
Option 1	3	6	17	3	2	–
Option 2	–	–	3	1	–	–
Labour						
Option 1	–	–	1	1	–	–
Option 2	–	–	–	–	–	–
Voluntary						
Option 1	–	1	4	1	–	–
Option 2	–	–	–	–	–	–

Business Sector

	Primary	Secondary	Tertiary	Omnibus
Option 1	6	12	4	9
Option 2	–	2	–	2

A look at the regional breakdown shows that 32 (74.4 percent) of the briefs were from Central Canadian organizations. This is significant because this is the manufacturing hub of Canada. A sectoral breakdown reveals that 70 percent of the relevant briefs are from the secondary sector. This evidence supports the notion that the preservation of an economic union is more important to the manufacturing interests in Canada, which are mostly located in Central Canada, than to the resource sector industries. The reason for this lies, at least partly in the fact that the bulk of manufactured goods produced in Ontario and Quebec are distributed within Canada. However, the fact that only 43 briefs even address the question, despite the fact that it is a major preoccupation of the Commission, suggests that intervenors perceive this as a distinctly secondary matter.

REGIONAL DEVELOPMENT POLICY

Briefs which make specific reference to policies that promote development in certain areas of the country were examined. Two categories were created: those groups that support location-specific policies (Option 1), and those that express opposition to them (Option 2).

	Business	Labour	Voluntary
Option 1	11	6	3
Option 2	8	–	–

Region

	Atlantic	Quebec	Ontario	Prairies	B.C.	Terr.
Business						
Option 1	4	2	2	–	1	2
Option 2	–	4	3	–	1	–
Labour						
Option 1	3	1	–	1	–	1
Option 2	–	–	–	–	–	–
Voluntary						
Option 1	–	–	2	–	1	–
Option 2	–	–	–	–	–	–

Business Sector

	Primary	Secondary	Tertiary	Omnibus
Option 1	2	0	1	8
Option 2	1	1	3	3

Only a small number of organizations actually address this issue. Some support for regional policies comes from all three categories of intervenors: business, labour and voluntary. All of the opposition, however, is from the business community, which is quite divided on the issue. Following is an excerpt from one of the business briefs that oppose regional development policies:

> The forest industry recognizes the need to redress regional disparities, but believes that the goal should be to devote our resources to industries in which Canada can be competitive.
>
> (*Council of Forest Industries of B.C.*, Transcript, Vancouver, September 8, 1983 [vol. 3], p. 523)

There is some support for regional development policies in all regions of the country. The only opposition, however, comes from Central Canada. Eleven of the business briefs support regional policies and seven express opposition. However, these seven form a majority of the briefs from Ontario and Quebec.

The six labour and the three voluntary sector briefs that address the issue of regional policies all support such efforts. These results are similar to those found in the analysis of the briefs addressing the concept of an industrial strategy. There is evidence of cleavages between regions of the country — primarily centre/periphery — and between business, on the one hand, and labour/voluntary sectors, on the other.

Senate Reform

A final issue concerns the reform of the institutions of the federal government, primarily the Senate. In particular, we were interested in those groups that view Senate reform as a means to ensure greater regional input into the federal decision-making process. Those briefs that mention Senate reform were classified according to one of two positions: reform as a means of increasing regional or provincial representation in Ottawa (Option 1) versus reform for a purpose other than the increase of regional input (Option 2).

	Business	Labour	Voluntary
Option 1	13	–	1
Option 2	5	1	3

Region

	Atlantic	Quebec	Ontario	Prairies	B.C.	Terr.
Business						
Option 1	3	1	2	7	–	–
Option 2	–	1	4	–	–	–
Labour						
Option 1	–	–	–	–	–	–
Option 2	–	–	–	–	1	–
Voluntary						
Option 1	–	–	–	1	–	–
Option 2	1	–	2	–	–	–

Business Sector

	Primary	Secondary	Tertiary	Omnibus
Option 1	2	1	3	7
Option 2	0	2	3	0

The results show that Senate reform was discussed by eighteen of the business groups, by one of the labour organizations and by four of the voluntary groups. Although the number of briefs addressing this issue is not large, of those that do, there is a regional difference of opinion concerning the purpose of Senate reform.

All but one of the briefs from the Atlantic provinces and from the Prairie provinces that mention Senate reform (Option 1) advocate reform at least partly for the purpose of increasing regional or provincial representation in Ottawa. Only a minority of the briefs from Central Canada (three of ten) mention this as a reason for reforming the Senate.

The other briefs that advocate reform of the Senate mention aspects other than regional or provincial representation. Other ideas include: making the Senate a body of permanent inquiry (*Confédération des caisses populaires*); maintaining it as a locus of thorough policy review (*Board of Trade of Metropolitan Toronto* (Transcript, Toronto, December 2, 1983 [vol. 56], p. 11952); putting scientists or other experts into the Senate (*Frank Maine*, Brief, October 31, 1983, p. 3) and simply making it more responsive (*Canadian Electrical Distributors Association*, Brief, October 6, 1983, p. 8).

Three of the voluntary sector briefs (*Fédération des francophones hors Québec, Council of National Ethnocultural Organizations, Fédération acadienne de la Nouvelle Écosse* (Transcript, Halifax, October 13, 1983 [vol. 24], p. 4651) and one of the business briefs (*Pierre Tremblay*, Transcript, Hull, December 13, 1983 [vol. 69], p. 14311) support reforming the Senate to make it more representative of either the dual nature or the ethnic composition of Canada.

Only one labour brief addresses the issue of the Senate, and it advocates that the Senate be abolished (*Victoria Labour Council*, Transcript, Victoria, September 15, 1983 [vol. 9], p. 2195).

GOVERNMENT VIEWPOINT

All four of the Atlantic provincial governments make specific reference to the Canadian economic union. While all decry barriers to trade and support the principle of an economic union, Prince Edward Island acknowledges that its support is qualified:

> Our concern is that with complete economic union comes an increased vulnerability. Our basic position is that given the present economic and political configuration in Canada, a reliance on market forces is likely to intensify regional problems.
>
> (*Government of Prince Edward Island*, Brief, December 2, 1983, p. 36)

Comments by the federal government representatives concerning regional development policy favour the principle of "region-specific" policies based on the different needs of different regions. For example, Lloyd Axworthy acknowledges that:

> . . . the western region's distance from the economic and population centres of Canada necessitates some reassurance and perhaps some guarantees that Westerners will be compensated because of the problems of geography, distance and lack of population. (Winnipeg — Day 1, p. 10874)

Several of the provinces address the issue of regional development. None opposes policies aimed at removing disparities among regions of the country. The Alberta government, for example, acknowledges this as an appropriate role for government (*Government of Alberta*, Brief, October 31, 1983, p. 11).

The Newfoundland, Nova Scotia and Prince Edward Island governments are all critical of various aspects of federal policy. All are concerned that the federal government has been retreating from its commitment to regional development objectives. The Atlantic provinces emphasize the importance of regional development policy. The Ontario government's brief supports the principle of removing regional disparities, but warns:

> In a period of slower growth and structural change, it is imperative that regional economic development programs — and, indeed, the full range of economic and fiscal policies aimed at encouraging growth — accentuate areas of comparative advantages and not foster, through subsidization, the growth of inefficient industries in economically disadvantaged regions.
>
> (*Government of Ontario*, Brief, December 2, 1983, p. 9)

With respect to the issue of the Senate, two (former) federal cabinet ministers advocate reform to make it more representative of the regions (Lloyd Axworthy, Senator Jack Austin). Four of the provincial governments address the issue of Senate reform, although each has a unique perspective. Alberta's view is similar to that espoused by the federal government, arguing that reform of the Senate must ensure a greater degree of sensitivity to regional and provincial objectives. Prince Edward Island is primarily concerned with establishing the principle of provincial equality in the Senate. The Ontario government supports the concept of making all central institutions more regionally sensitive but prefers to focus on the House of Commons, being wary of an elected Senate. Lastly, New Brunswick seems to oppose substantial reform of the Senate, objecting both to an elected Senate and to one appointed by the provinces.

Conclusions

Importance of Issues

The relative importance of certain issues to the interest groups may be determined simply by calculating the number of groups that chose to mention them. The results of this analysis suggest that many of the issues studied are not as important to some of the groups in society as is often thought.

Concern over federal-provincial relations is possibly one example. Perhaps the most significant point coming out of the examination of perceptions about intergovernmental relations is the small number of briefs which address this issue. Regarding the business sector, substantially greater proportions of organizations addressed the issues of government intervention, foreign investment and even the economic union than addressed federal-provincial interaction.

The Salience of Regionalism

A regional breakdown of the organizations that submitted briefs reveals that 12.3 percent were from the Atlantic region, 13.5 percent from Quebec, 38.5 percent from Ontario, 19.8 percent from the Prairie provinces, 13 percent from British Columbia and 2.6 percent from the Territories. This compares to the population, which is distributed as follows: 9.1 percent from the Atlantic region, 26.2 percent from Quebec, 35.4 percent from Ontario, 17.6 percent from the Prairie provinces, 11.3 percent from B.C. and 0.3 percent from the Territories.

One of the key objectives of the analysis of the briefs presented to the Commission was to determine the salience of regionalism. The examination reveals evidence of three distinct types of regionalism in the perceptions of Canadian interest groups.

First, there are certain issues that tend to elicit responses along regional lines. Some of the issues upon which there is a clear divergence of opinion do reveal regional cleavages. In particular, opinions on regional development policy and Senate reform seem to be at least partly shaped by geographical location.

The briefs that address this issue of regional development policy were primarily from the Atlantic region or the Territories, where these policies are overwhelmingly endorsed, or from Central Canada (Ontario and Quebec), where the majority express opposition to such policies. Concerning the issue of the Senate, nearly all Western and Atlantic groups that advocate reform do so, at least partly, for the purpose of increasing the regional or provincial voice in Ottawa. A majority of the relevant groups from Ontario and Quebec, however, do not mention this as a reason for reforming the Senate.

Second, certain other issues illustrate regionalism in a more subtle fashion. Some issues seem more or less likely to be addressed by a group depending on the region where it is located. For example, a greater proportion of the briefs addressing the issues of the economic union (74.4 percent), federal-provincial relations (78.8 percent), and foreign investment in Canada (75.5 percent) were from Central Canada than was the proportion of briefs from this region in the overall total (52.0 percent). (See Appendix A.) Furthermore, 27.8 percent of the briefs addressing decentralization and 25 percent of those concerning regional development policy were from the Atlantic region, even though this region submitted only 12.3 percent of the total briefs. This suggests that these two issues are of particular importance for groups in this region.

A third aspect looks at regionalism from a different perspective. In addition to seeking to determine if "region" is a factor in predicting either what is important (i.e., worth mentioning) or which position an interest group holds on a particular issue, here the concern is to determine if "region" holds as a self-identifying concept.

This is of particular interest in this study since the terms of reference of the Commission tend not to invite regional representations. Very few of the groups that submitted briefs or appeared before the Commission are primarily territorial. Most represent an economic sector or special interest not defined in regional terms. Municipalities and provincial and territorial governments are obvious exceptions. Regional development agencies and local-level chambers of commerce are also somewhat "territorial," although they represent areas that are significantly smaller than the Canadian regions as conventionally understood. It is fair to say in general that it is the economic or special interest consideration of most groups rather than the territorial one which predominantes in the briefs. Most groups do not speak in terms of a "regional interest."

One notable exception to this rule concerns groups from the Atlantic region. Several organizations from this region, representing diverse interests, refer to the "Atlantic region" and, more often than not, to its poor position in Canada and its need for special attention. Following are two examples. (Further evidence of this trend can be found in Appendix B.)

> For too long the Atlantic Region has been a womb for industrial Canada. We suggest a reassessment of those national policies which artificially support an industrial base in Central Canada.
>
> (*Dartmouth Chamber of Commerce*, Brief, October 3, 1983, p. 16)

> We have found in the past that Central Canada's attitude towards us and by extension of the Federal Government's attitude towards us, to be very paternalistic. This, in turn, is reflected in the political decisions which are made affecting the Maritimes.
>
> (*City of Charlottetown*, Brief, September 14, 1983, p. 6)

Cross-Regional Cleavages

While there is evidence of regionalism being salient with respect to some specific issues, certain of the other issues examined tend to divide Canadian society along lines other than region. There was a divergence of opinion, for example, with respect to issues such as an industrial strategy, decentralization and foreign investment. Opinions on these matters tend to divide groups along non-regional cleavages, such as big versus small business or labour versus business.

The briefs were broken down into categories: business, labour and voluntary sectors. Furthermore, the business organizations were subdivided into primary, secondary and tertiary sectors. The findings suggest that certain issues do tend to divide according to one or other of these cleavages. For example, while over half of the business organizations support the least interventionist position for government (Option 1), all of the labour groups advocate a greater role for government in the economy (Options 2 or 3).

Support for greater decentralization comes primarily from representatives for small business. While business is divided on the issue of foreign
investment and control, briefs from labour and voluntary groups mostly
are opposed to the extent of foreign control in Canada. A similar division occurs with respect to the issue of an industrial strategy. Of the groups
which mention this, nearly all of the labour and voluntary representatives
favour such a strategy, while the business community is split.

One other cleavage of particular interest is foreign multinational versus domestic corporations. It is difficult to comment on the strength of
this distinction because of the paucity of briefs from foreign multinational
corporations. It seems that the few foreign multinational corporations
which did make presentations to the Commission tend to coalesce around
certain positions. Generally, the multinationals show a preference for the
federal government, favouring a reliance on market forces, opposing
regional development policy, and appealing for clear and consistent direction from government. The following excerpts appear to be typical of the
briefs submitted by the multinational corporations:

> We have found government policy to be inconsistent, at times contradictory,
> and not responsive.   (*Celanese Canada Inc.*, Brief, November 4, 1983, p. 10)

> Governments ought to be facilitators of change rather than architects of
> change. Policies and regulations should create conditions favourable to
> economic growth, leaving it to private enterprise and the free market system
> to do the job . . . it is best suited to do: to reward efficiency and eliminate
> inefficiency, thus maximizing productivity, growth and the real income of
> our people.   (*George Weston Ltd.*, Brief, November 4, 1983, p. 5)

While these positions are not unlike those held by many Canadian companies, the perceptions of the domestic firms are far less homogeneous
than the foreign multinationals.

On some of the more important issues being addressed by the Commission, there seems to be a congruence of opinion across Canada. These
include: a need for increased and more effective consultation between interest groups and governments and an exasperation with federal-provincial
fighting. These may be considered as motherhood issues in Canada, and
as such there is little or no opposition expressed.

Government Viewpoint

The cursory examination of the government briefs which address the issues
analyzed here does not lead to any firm conclusions about government
policy vis-à-vis the positions of Canadian interest groups. Much like the
interest groups themselves, the governments in Canada seem to hold a
variety of positions concerning many of the issues being examined.

It seems that the positions of the provincial governments reflect both
the ideological colour of the governing party and the geographical loca-

tion of the province. As a result, the issues that seem to divide the interest groups along regional lines also tend to divide the provincial governments. On these issues, the perspectives of the provincial governments tend to be aligned with the dominant position of the interest groups in their region (for example, the positions of the Maritime governments on regional development policy and the Alberta government with respect to Senate reform).

Some Reflections

Some final remarks should be made regarding the nature of the briefs themselves. The first concerns the absence of several major actors in the Canadian economy from the ranks of those who either submitted briefs or appeared before the Commission. This suggests that there may have been a certain problem of the perceived legitimacy of the Commission itself, especially within the business community. There may have been a feeling that the Commission was too closely linked with the governing federal (Liberal) party, and the days of that government were generally thought to be numbered. Perhaps some businessmen thought it futile to make representation. They no doubt recalled previous consultations with business as part of the Enterprise 77 operation, when the Department of Industry, Trade and Commerce attempted to consult the business community on questions of economic policy in 1977. Then, the business community revealed considerable exasperation with government. When business cooperated in the Tier I and Tier II process in 1978, business leaders well recall, this initiative was never followed up. Both of these operations demanded great efforts from and inconvenience for the country's business leaders and their experiences engendered a feeling that government tended to be ready to ask for advice but was not at all disposed to act upon it. Some business leaders were suspicious that the government's motives and concerns were mainly manoeuvres to secure electoral advantage for themselves and the party then in power, which by then had forfeited the confidence of the business community.

Of those groups which did present briefs to the Commission, it seems that many were somewhat divided over what to say and, therefore, were unable to make clear or strong recommendations, or else did not take the exercise very seriously. This tone seems to be reflected in some of the briefs and presentations. As a result, these briefs tend to be full of generalizations, containing few insights or developed analyses. Moreover, they usually fail to address many of the issues that were of concern to this study.

Particularly significant is the virtual absence of a key and leading element of the Canadian business community, namely, the multinational corporations. This may be a reaction to their perception of the nationalism of a Liberal government that had enacted FIRA and the National Energy Program, and then promised to strengthen the former and implement an industrial strategy for Canada. These moves may well have led the leaders of the multinationals to choose to avoid the risks of becoming involved with a Commission to develop further policy for that government: better to sit on their hands and move their support to the Conservatives in anticipation of a new government. (*The Financial Post* reported that over 80 percent of corporate chief executive officers favoured the Conservatives in the 1984 election.) The most seriously alienated of all these large multinational industries, the petroleum industry, did very little indeed. (Only one submitted a brief.) This attitude of reticence was shared by Canadian big business as well: witness the failure to participate of the major of these, the steel industry.

This should not be considered surprising. Business interests are primarily concerned to have an environment which facilitates investor confidence. The general attitude and posture of government was not generally acceptable to business, so there was little disposition to launch a concerted campaign to change it. A wiser strategy seemed to be simply to react passively and await the opportunities that the near future seemed to offer. The failure of the private sector to address issues such as the economic union and federal-provincial relations suggests that it does not consider these to be serious problems, as they are currently being handled by government leaders. The implication is that the status quo is generally acceptable. Policies in Canada, with some notable exceptions, have generally satisfied the self-regarding interests of business.

Chapter 6

The Two Dynamics:
Crosscutting and Reinforcing —
Assessment and Remedies

Asymmetry: The Canadian Interest Group System and Federal-Provincial Relations

Canadians are accustomed to hearing complaints about the cost of federalism and the inevitable inefficiency caused by duplication in and differences between the two levels of government. While of course there is truth here, the fact remains that federalism is, for Canada, the price of union. Any serious suggestion to change the distribution of powers in the direction of legislative union for Canada would immediately be resisted in Quebec, and if persisted in, would lead to the separation of that province. Sovereignty association may not be an acute issue at the moment, but it could very quickly become revitalized if the federal government were to attempt significantly to enhance its powers at the expense of the provinces.

One cannot be quite as confident in referring to the other outlying regions, the West and the Atlantic provinces. However, as the conflicts of the past ten years have shown, they have come to resent and actively resist an Ottawa-Toronto power axis. There can be no doubt that any diminution in their autonomy would add to their feeling of alienation and, therefore, might set in motion another round of intergovernmental conflict. Federalism for Canada has been the indispensable precondition for the national union. Designed in the beginning as a safeguard for the linguistic and cultural autonomy of Quebec, federalism has become the bulwark of Canada's socio-economic diversity.

Federalism has meant that the people in the provinces, by electing their own legislative assemblies, are creating defensive mechanisms to protect themselves from the Canadian majority outside their own jurisdictions. This gives a feeling of security which permits active participation in pan-Canadian politics.

Indeed federalism, with the elaborate system of equalization and stabilization of provincial revenues that has been put in place, has permitted a substantial level of standardization of government services across the country. In terms of lifestyle and standard of services, the variance between provinces has declined considerably. If Canada is "becoming less, rather than more, diverse,"[1] federalism clearly is not an absolute obstacle to such developments, although there is no doubt that it, in some aspects, poses problems. Certainly it does influence the way in which communities perceive themselves and render services to their citizens. The growing similarities in the standards of services that Canadians receive and in the way they experience government have not been accompanied by declines in regional or provincial feeling. It appears somewhat of a paradox that in a time when these conditions are more similar than they have ever been, there is evidence of serious tension. Perhaps as governments become increasingly important in the lives of citizens, and as the political process calls forth more extravagant promises, people's expectations from government grow greater than the ability of governments to satisfy these expectations. The result is disappointment, and in a federal system such disappointment can readily be canalized into feelings of dissatisfaction with the federal government in relieving problems within the regions.

There are numerous interest groups seeking to influence both the provincial governments and the federal government. Naturally, they are concerned to position themselves and to structure their organizations in order to facilitate their work in influencing government. The governments are established institutions with given instrumentalities. The interest groups must adapt themselves to these, and they do so. Since Canada is a federal state, it should not be surprising that interest groups tend to be organized to facilitate interaction with both levels of government. This has meant, in most cases, either a federal structure or a confederal one in which the major power rests in the provincial or regional offices. Once a system is operating with communications passing back and forth between interest groups and governments, then each side inevitably influences the other in a reciprocal pattern of interaction. It is difficult to make generalizations in this area because the groups are not bound by rules as to their own internal organization and conduct. They organize themselves in the way that they individually perceive to be most advantageous and effective. Also, each confronts its unique problems. Some groups, for example, represent industries that are engaged in the exploitation of provincial natural resources. Their primary relationship is bound to be with the provincial governments. To defend this relationship, they are often led to defend their province in disputes with the federal government and other bodies. However, they are also careful not to be totally committed to one government, because this would put them in a dangerous and vulnerable position. It is in the interest of a group to have friends in all governments and on all sides. However, when choices have to be made, as they sometimes do, the groups are often compelled to opt in favour of the government with the greatest concern in their area of activity and with the greatest power over them. The provincial governments in the case of natural resource industries are the best example. A similar vulnerability exists in the case of federally chartered or regulated industries, which must be mindful of the predominant power of the federal government. They, of course, are cautious not to come into open conflict with that government, which they are anxious to influence and keep on friendly terms. Examples are the banks, the railways and the major transnational airlines. Since some of these are federal Crown corporations, a close relationship with the federal government is inevitable.

Sometimes the accusation is made that interest groups attempt to play governments off, one against another. This is an easy accusation to make and a difficult one to demonstrate. In fact, it is dangerous for interest groups to engage in such behaviour openly, because governments can always retaliate against those who declare themselves their enemies. The real situation is one in which groups do not declare themselves as the allies of any one government. To do so is to lose their bargaining power and their independence. This, in turn, means they will try to maintain civil relations with any and all governments, and the nature of the relationship in any particular case will depend on the particular circumstances uniting it with the respective government.

At the one extreme are those groups that have the bulk of their relations with only one level of government — the examples already cited. Others maintain continuing relations with both levels. The nature of the relationship, however, changes as the circumstances of the respective issues change. For example, when major industrial organizations are considering making an important investment and are looking for a suitable location, they possess great power. In such conditions it is not uncommon for several provinces in Canada, as well as some other governments in other countries, to court the industry seeking to attract that investment. This is the kind of situation which has drawn forth the accusation about "playing off governments against each other." In their attempts to attract investment, governments are likely to offer concessions as enticements. These might include subsidies to support planned construction, improvements in transportation facilities, and may even go so far as to involve promises of legislation relating to trade union power or labour costs. Corporations that receive such inducements could well be perceived as playing off one government against another. However, the relationship is really inherent in the situation. Each side is behaving as one would expect it to behave in order to maximize its own advantages. If the enticements are successful, the government offering the most attractive terms is likely to succeed in seeing the investment made within its borders.

However, once the investment has been made, the plant built and operations are underway, then the ability of the corporation to demand concessions decreases, and the power of the government over it increases. The relationship becomes more equal because the industry has its own investment to protect, although, of course, it reserves the decision as to where its future commitments will be made. Governments on the other hand have an industry within their territory which can be taxed and, in some ways, regulated and controlled. However there are limits. In the extreme, the industry always reserves the right to close down the plant, thereby creating serious political problems for the government through unemployment and reduced economic activity.

Once a substantial investment pattern has developed within a government's area of jurisdiction, there is a substantial commitment on the part of both the government and the industry to the well-being of that industrial sector. The two sides become allies in dealing with outside jurisdictions (other provinces or the federal government). This has created a situation in which certain provinces have become clearly identified with a given industry. The classic cases are Alberta with the oil and gas industry; Ontario with secondary manufacturing in general and the automobile industry in particular; Quebec with textiles, clothing, furniture and other labour intensive industries; the sea coast industries with British Columbia and the Atlantic provinces, and so on. Very often circumstances arise in which the interest of one of these particular industries may be perceived as conflicting with interests outside the province or with the national interest as a whole. The classic example here is the question of the pricing of petroleum products. There was an obvious conflict between the interests of Alberta and the other producer provinces, on the one hand, and Ontario and the other user provinces on the other. Since the issue was subject to governmental regulation, this brought the governments of both producing and consuming provinces into confrontation with the federal government, which had jurisdictional control over the interprovincial movement of goods, and a general power to levy taxes. As it turned out, the federal government became a virtual arbiter between the interests of these two regions of Canada, as reflected in the interests of the industries concerned. In such circumstances, "God is on the side of the bigger battalions." The federal government is bound to be more sensitive to the demands of the most populous and influential part of Canada.

This basic and to all intents and purposes inevitable fact in part accounts for the growing feeling of alienation in the outlying regions, where populations are smaller than in Central Canada. As government becomes involved in ever more aspects of the life of Canadians, the likelihood of such complaints is bound to increase. In this process, the interest groups simply mobilize their forces and represent their interests in order to maximize their chances of success. What such situations reveal is each government being mobilized to represent the major organized interests within its borders. Conflicts between these interests take on a federal-provincial dimension when the federal government is compelled to take a position that brings it into conflict with one or more of the provinces. As noticed in Chapter 4, when the issue shifts to the federal-provincial level, there is sometimes a tendency for the interest groups to be frozen-out, as the governments seek to reconcile the question between themselves in a way that will do each government the least harm. However, when the situation is looked at from a distance, one must also consider that the governments involved in the issue would likely remain faithful to the interests with which they had been identified in the past. The fact that groups were not actively involved in the last stages of reconciliation does not mean that their interests were not protected. Relationships between governments and groups are long-standing and deep and reflect profound realities, and the fact that the group represents a significant part of the provincial economy is bound to lead the provincial government to act as its champion and the champion of the people who work for it.

The asymmetry of the Canadian interest group structure, as it relates to the different levels of government, is twofold. As indicated above, there are substantial interests traditionally linked to the federal government, such as transportation and finance, and there are dominant Central Canadian industrial interests located in Ontario which are "naturally" closer to the levers of power in Ottawa than are the resource-based industries and interests in the peripheral areas. At the same time, however, substantial economic interests are closely linked to provincial governments, such as the energy-related industries in Alberta, and the entire complex of socioeconomic province-building in Quebec. (See Chapter 2.)

The Canadian socioeconomic structure is highly regionalized. There is an inevitable tension between the manufacturing interests of the Central region and the resource-based ones in the outlying regions. This has been increased by the fact that foreign capital built up regional and sectoral north-south patterns of transnational economic interdependence, which cut across the earlier pattern of east-west socioeconomic and industrial integration. Ideally, the federal government should be the arbiter of the tensions and conflicts arising from this asymmetrical relationship. However, this federal role of arbitration has seldom been seriously pursued, and for fairly obvious reasons. For one, the federal government was designed originally to facilitate the development of the periphery, and not to have it compete with Central Canadian interests. Secondly, the federal government became deeply involved with foreign investor interests. And finally, an incomplete set of representative federal institutions (the Senate, for example, never really spoke for provincial interests) did not equip the federal government to carry out an arbitration role.

It would be next to impossible to offer an assessment of the overall distribution and allocation of the power and influence of organized interests with regard to the different levels of government. The picture is a confused morass of relationships of the many interest groups. Some are identified with the federal government and others with one or more provincial governments. Mostly there are shifting relationships with both levels, with some groups close to one department of a given government while at the same time involved in tense relations with another department of the same government. It would therefore be simplistic to say that federal-provincial conflict stems solely from a pattern of unilateral centre-periphery dependency; but it would likewise be inappropriate to dismiss all federal-provincial conflict as substantially meaningless in the light of the dominant (and as some would say, largely foreign-owned) capital interests.

Complex industrial systems are inevitably characterized by a polycentric structure of primary (resource-based), secondary (manufacturing) and tertiary (administration and information controlling) economic activities. The typical pattern in Canada involves a large spatial separation of primary and secondary activities. The crucial point, however, is the central concentration of the tertiary sector, which tends to be spatially separated from primary and secondary activities.

Those aspects of the tertiary sector dealing with the transmission of information, instructions and orders over space, tend in Canada to be concentrated in the Toronto-Ottawa-Montreal head office complex. This leaves Canada in the same situation as Britain and France with a concentrated economic nerve centre, but contrasting with Germany and Switzerland, which have spatially separated economic nerve centres.

The incongruence of tertiary sector concentration and organized interest segmentation poses a fundamental problem with regard to the harmonization and coordination of the Canadian national economy. The oft-heard accusation that organized interest groups can successfully play the two levels of government off one against another seems less plausible than the assertion that only those interests can be successful that have established a substantial degree of access to the central command activities. However, given the ambiguity of the constitutional distribution of powers, especially with regard to the salient energy and resource sectors, these centralized activities must rely on the outcome of federal-provincial negotiation.[2]

A large part of interest intermediation in Canada is therefore, for better or for worse, tied to the process of intergovernmental relations. The assumption that intergovernmental bargaining tends to become detached from legitimate interest input (the frozen-out thesis) gains plausibility when we consider that at times governments have to set deadlines to reach decisions. Modern international economic interdependence often compels governments to give rapid responses. Incongruence between interest structures and decision-making structures leads to policy immobilism. As Richard Simeon pointed out, ". . . listening to all the grievances, one sometimes gets the impression that all regions are 'losers' in the Confederation balance sheet" (Simeon, 1979, p. 7). This raises the question as to the political legitimacy of the present state of intergovernmental relations and as to its asymmetrical responses to the organized interests of Canadian society.

Elite Accommodation and Federalism

From the outset, the Canadian federal union was designed to accommodate certain dominant business interests concerned with development based on railways. Policy making has remained largely in the hands of a circumscribed socioeconomic policy community composed of senior government officials, leading politicians (mainly ministers), and the leaders of the major economic interest groups (large corporations and some other organized interests). This tends to favour business over other parts of the community, despite the addition of very strong central agencies. It still reflects the values and preferences of the highly educated decision makers.

Canadian policy-making mechanisms are "two or three steps removed from any sort of popular control," as a result of the workings of executive federalism (Panitch, 1979, p. 11) and also of the mechanisms by which organized interests influence and interact with the two levels of government. There is a double cost for democratic legitimacy: one is the result of an elitist style of political accommodation which brings together the political leaders (ministers) and the relatively poorly legitimated managers of private institutions and organizations. This bias is enhanced by the high degree of selectivity as to who has access to these negotiations, most of which take place behind closed doors.

Given the incremental nature of such interest group politics, especially considering that the entire process is repeated to a certain extent because of the existence of two levels of government with substantial jurisdictional authority, there is an inherent bias against overall economic planning and the coordination of government activity. Instead, there are eleven systems of incremental policy making. The secrecy of the negotiation processes becomes a provocation for the excluded groups, undermining harmony within the country and encouraging them to engage in confrontation strategies. Because government tends to "side with the strong against the weak" (in Robert Presthus's words), the character of politics is led to become non-consensual and confrontational.

What are the consequences of this? First, the confrontations characterizing a society fragmented by economic sector and geography create an atmosphere of inflexibility and disillusionment which can paralyze the policy-making dynamic. They reinforce status quo thinking in politics and they erect barriers between the privileged groups with access to government and the others who are largely on the outside. The process immobilizes society and divides it between the pro–status quo position of the privileged parts, on the one hand, and the rising demands and needs of the rest of the community, on the other. In times of economic scarcity and financial constraint, the entire system becomes more unmanageable. While this problem of "ungovernability" besets all advanced industrial democracies

(Crozier et al., 1975), it is reinforced in federal systems such as the Canadian one, when the immobilism of interest group accommodation encounters federal-provincial disagreement, producing near-paralysis.

Second, and more discouraging, the general degree of inflexibility and deadlock leads to a reductionist reaction among participants of the elite community. Policy options tend to be defined incrementally, with those most likely to preserve the status quo preferred over those which seem to involve more far-reaching adjustments in the longer-term national interest. These tend not be be seriously considered, because they do not have the endorsement of a cautious and defensive elite community. The tendency is for meaningful participation in the policy-making process to be limited to those interests which have a substantive interest in the issues under discussion. Therefore, there is an inevitable bias against change, which is a drag on the adaptive capacity of the government to meet challenges. Problems tend to be defined narrowly and in a technical way. This further excludes the non-expert part of the community (non-expert as defined by the dominant interests).

Third, this results in a considerable waste of scarce resources. The brokerage incentives of governments lead them into policies of financial overcommitment and deficit financing to support the status quo. While it is generally assumed that these deficits stem from the governments' succumbing to the exaggerated and ever-growing welfare expectations of the general public, a recent study has demonstrated that a major source of the Canadian deficit is the tax reduction policies and incentives granted to the business community by hard-pressed governments anxious to re-establish business confidence and satisfactory investment climate.[3]

Fourth, the recent appearance of new interest groups to protest the dominance of the older institutionalized (and mainly business-oriented) ones has placed government in a position in which it is pushed in two directions and forced to make hard choices. The newer groups, oriented to issues, or speaking for previously unrepresented elements, lack the privileged access to government of the institutionalized ones, but now have the power to reach the public through dramatic demonstrations carried on television and in other media. This provides a fertile ground for the growth of new social movements and the formation of organized interests. Such special interest groups as women's organizations, native people's organizations, senior citizens' groups and organized ethnic groups have begun to challenge the vested interests which employ elite accommodation methods. There are several explanations for this new tendency — notably the change in values of some elements in the community and the deterioration of traditional belief systems, which seem to have affected all advanced industrial societies (Inglehart, 1977). Other reasons are the availability of the new electronic media to display and demonstrate these groups' grievances and demands. Also, the general climate of economic constraint affects and mobilizes these peripheral groups more than the established interest organizations.

Governments now are compelled to respond to these pressures. Embarrassed by reports of the bias of some of the particular groups which had been a major source of information for governments, they had to develop their own expertise, information and skills in order to protect themselves from being misled. They had to establish new institutions and to revive old ones in order to deal with the pressures created by these problems. In a way, this has given governments a new degree of autonomy: the pressures from the established interest groups are politically confronted and, to a certain extent, contained by the pressures of the newer groups speaking for the previously excluded. The traditional networks of elite accommodation have tended to concentrate less attention on the executive in recent years, or they have been less successful in their attempts. As James Gillies pointed out, business has to find new paths and to adapt to these new realities of policy making in the democratic state (Gillies, 1981).

The fifth and last consequence to be mentioned as a result of the asymmetrical politics of confrontation in Canadian federalism, is the growing autonomy of the state. Labelled as the "other crisis of Canadian federalism" (Cairns, 1979), the growth of government at both levels results partly from confrontation between governments over jurisdiction and partly from cleavages between regional interests. Now governments can play off the pressures of the conflicting interests to which they are subjected, one against another. On the other hand, however, the new freedom conferred on government by the erection of countervailing pressures is, in a sense, rendered useless by the budgetary restrictions resulting from economic scarcity and from the greater expectations and demands of an enlarged interest community. The result is government policies, which may succeed in maintaining through compromise some degree of community consensus but fall far short of dealing effectively with issues, or satisfying the interest groups.

In short, the Canadian political system appears to be confronted by a double problem: one of the performance of institutions of decision making at both levels, and one of intergovernmental relations. Clearly, there is a declining capacity to manage the economy. Given the international economic turbulence of the present time with its effects on markets for Canadian products, every attempt by government to stabilize and assist the important sectors of the Canadian economy seems to lead to disruption of the peripheral parts of the economy, thereby increasing their demands for compensatory action. This is of course not a problem confined to Canada; it has been aptly described as "the contradiction of late capitalist systems (Offe, 1984, pp. 125–29).

On the intergovernmental front, there seems to be a growing separation of form and content. While the need for coordination and collaboration between governments was never greater, the actual situation is one where the governments are peculiarly unable to attain this objective. Consequently, any attempt at reforming the central institutions of Canadian federalism must primarily focus on the modes of accommodation through which organized interests could be harmonized and coordinated directly with the process of intergovernmental relations itself. This is a problem of interorganizational decision making.

Interorganizational Decision Making in Complex Industrial Systems

There is a growing separation of form from content in modern democratic systems. The traditional institutions of representative democracy are being bypassed, as important political decisions are increasingly being reached through direct negotiations between government and important organized interest groups — most notably business and labour organizations, the related banking sector, and some other significant organized interests, such as farmers' organizations. Another aspect is the growing public sector, when governments run and control large public enterprises themselves (such as the Canadian Crown corporations).

Apart from the direct involvement of the large and dominant organized interests in policy making, the process of intergovernmental decision making itself increasingly bypasses the older, established constitutional forms of government. In Canada, the main obstacles to policy coordination lie in the incongruence of the federal-provincial bargaining mechanism and the asymmetrical interest group structure. Economic planning and harmonization are impeded by the fact that both governmental and interest structures are at the same time reinforcing and crosscutting. Moreover, the intergovernmental relations mechanisms tend to be unable to respond sufficiently to these overlapping interest group structures.

The connections between the business elites and the state are characterized more by their informality and fluidity than by a firm set of consultative mechanisms. The high degree of overlapping membership and career interchange between business interests and government sustains this informality (Clement, 1975). On the other hand, labour in Canada has never achieved the same degree of formalized status as in many Western European countries. More dependent on collective action than other interest groups because of its lack of bargaining power, the Canadian labour movement has largely failed to attain the status of a major national political force, and its leaders remain on the margin of the power structure of elite accommodation (Panitch, 1984). Major reasons for this are the fragmented and regionalized nature of the Canadian labour movement, reflecting the conditions of the economy, the traditionally less powerful situation of unions in North America than is the case in northern Europe, and the fact that the Canadian Labour Congress is affiliated with Canada's third party, the New Democratic Party.

As a consequence, what mechanisms of interorganizational decision making there are in Canada appear to be peculiarly unstructured and improvised. In the case of organized private interests, the main features are the fragmented state of the economy, the domination of business interests and their confrontation with the new issue-oriented interest organizations, and the fact that many of the crucial business decisions are made outside the country. In the case of the political institutions, the lack of coordination is due to a number of factors: the fact that for lengthy periods since 1957 Canada has lacked a nation-wide governing party, which the September 1984 Conservative victory overcame; the lack of a strong regionally representative Senate; the strong connections between the province-building dynamic and business and capital interests outside the country; and the bias of the electoral system, which largely excludes parties close to the new social movements and grossly underrepresents the New Democrats, the party best equipped to speak for the labour movement.

The Canadian problem is the failure of the current institutional and conventional interest intermediation mechanisms to be integrated with the process of intergovernmental relations. The process of policy formation and decision making remains fragmented, incremental and opaque. Like the American system of clientelism, described by Theodore Lowi, it results in the "atrophy of institutions of popular control" and the "creation of new structures of privilege." It promotes stability and therefore rigidity at the expense of flexibility, and it ultimately undermines the legitimacy of the system (Lowi, 1979, pp. 58–63). A similar process has been noted in the case of Western Europe (Pizzorno, 1981). Political parties have been shifting more and more to become opportunistic catch-all parties, and they are increasingly unable to formulate coherent policies. As party programs are coming to resemble one another more and more, voters become increasingly disillusioned by the apparent lack of choice. Governments rely more and more on the input of interest groups, and they are consequently more exposed to their pressures for both expenditures and policy making. This situation contributes to the general crisis of governability in Canada and other advanced industrial democracies. The old pluralist system of policy making is not up to the strain of increased expectations and the demands which are often presented in non-negotiable form. As the political advantage and skill of the dominant interest groups enables them to prevail, the influence of the general citizenry comes to be contained, despite the new assertiveness of issue-oriented groups. Pluralist politics under these conditions lead to public attitudes of indifference, cynicism or pessimism. In response, governments are led to legitimize themselves by incorporating some of the groups into the decision-making process, so that they can be held responsible to some degree for policy outputs.

Turning to these new modes of interorganizational decision making at the same time increases the pressures under which governments have to operate. Coming to depend on organized interests, they have to satisfy both the dominant interest groups and the general public: the former through business support policies in order to restore business confidence and to regain international competitiveness; and the latter by maintaining, if not enlarging, the redistributive schemes of the welfare state. Enmeshed in the process of interorganizational bargaining, governments tend to become immobilized, and organized interests assume the role of rigid private governments. A paradox appears. While organized interests become politicized as primary actors in the process of policy formation, the very process of interorganizational decision making itself becomes depoliticized and remote from popular control.

It is nevertheless useful to examine the Western European experience with interorganizational decision making, insofar as it constitutes an attempt to develop formal relations between interest groups and government. It often includes direct participation in policy making and the working out of contractual formulas between the interest groups themselves. In recent years, a substantial body of literature has appeared which describes, analyzes and criticizes these arrangements. Best known and of primary interest for the analysis of policy formation in advanced industrial systems is the neocorporatist school.[4] These analyses have mainly focussed on the countries of northwestern continental Europe (Austria, West Germany, Holland and Sweden). Can Canada learn from the European corporatist experience?

Leo Panitch has aptly defined neocorporatism as "a political structure within advanced capitalism which integrates organized socioeconomic producer groups through a system of representation and cooperative mutual interaction at the leadership level, and mobilization and social control at the mass level" (Panitch, 1979a, p. 44). Philippe Schmitter's analysis (Schmitter, 1981) leads to the assumption that such corporatist arrangements are likely to be adopted as a remedy for the unruliness, "unstableness," and ineffectiveness of modern government. Some countries that have resorted to such arrangements appear to have lower rates of unemployment than others that have not done so. The objective of corporatist intermediation is to resolve the conflicts of society by taking its dominant group organizations into direct governmental consultation and to produce consensual policy. The dominant groups (usually business and labour organizations) gain access to the policy-making process but, in exchange, must accept constraints and restrictive obligations. They receive official status in exchange for commitments not to resort to "irresponsible" action. The strategic objective is to restrain trade union demands and to relieve overloaded government agendas from uncoordinated demands on the part of business interests. Mutual restraint, especially through incomes policy, is expected to stabilize and contain both unemployment and inflation.

As Claus Offe (1981) and others have shown, however, both the legitimacy and the efficacy of corporatist intermediation may be doubtful. As organized interests tend to undermine responsible parliamentary government, they may also impede efficient economic planning, and they may even contribute to inflation and structural unemployment. Conflicts between dominant interest groups at the level of government mediation have tended to be settled at the expense of the weaker groups and the unorganized. These, in turn, tend to redress the situation by organizing themselves. This leads to the next stage, in which pressure group cooperation with government is extended, and while this may reduce the potential for irresponsible behaviour on behalf of any particular group, at the same time it makes government even less flexible. The critics of neocorporatist arrangements in late capitalist societies have repeatedly emphasized that there is no "logic of exchange" in tripartism (Fach, 1983) and that neocorporatism, therefore, is only a continuation of the same old politics of inequality through extra-parliamentary means.

An even more serious criticism of the usefulness of corporatist interest intermediation is the recognition that it seems to work best in times of prosperity, i.e., when everybody can claim at least some sort of prize. On the other hand, it tends to break down in times of economic scarcity and crisis, i.e., precisely when most needed. Under such conditions, business interests are not likely to yield to union demands especially when the interests of both business and state elites are not contained by specific, distinctive party programs, and when the parliamentary representation of workers' interests is weak.

This is particularly the case in Canada, where the New Democratic Party has never shared in government at the federal level, and has formed the provincial government only in three of the Western provinces, for limited periods of time. There is substantial evidence that corporatist or tripartite arrangements have been most successful in countries with social democratic governments and/or societies with a high level of trade union organization, or other kinds of association. A tradition of consociational social organization is particularly favourable for neocorporatism, as are overlapping memberships and interlocking leadership circles between social organizations and political parties. Obviously, corporatist arrangements are more likely to be successful when they are supported by consensual compromises among similar configurations of interest within the political institutions and policy-making processes.

Canada ranks low among Western countries in its societal predisposition for corporatist arrangements, and so it has made few actual experiments with tripartism. Nevertheless, there have been some attempts. Before 1975, there were negotiations toward some form of tripartism between government, business and labour leaders. While these came to an abrupt end with the introduction of compulsory wage and price controls, there have been some discussions of such arrangements after those controls were lifted, most notably the collaborative initiatives of 1978 (Tier I and Tier II). As the introduction of compulsory wage and price controls indicates, the main obstacle to industrial tripartism in Canada may very well be the country's somewhat competitive and conflict-prone political culture, characterized by the close association of big government and big business, with no organized counterpart on the side of labour. On the other hand, it is the political culture of conflict-avoidance which has facilitated corporatism in countries like West Germany — at least until the general economic crisis struck, leading to the breakdown of the spirit of conciliatory agreement.

In Canada the pervading American example, in part through the multinational corporations, ties the pattern of industrial relations to the American way, which has so far largely eschewed corporatist solutions. As many of the key industries and business organizations in Canada are branches of multinational corporations, it is more difficult for Canadian governments to reach binding agreements with them than would be the case with Canadian-owned and controlled enterprises. On the labour side conditions are even less propitious for corporatism. Canadian labour is weaker and much more divided than its counterpart in Nordic Europe and encompasses a much smaller portion of the labour force. It is affiliated with a party that is always in opposition at Ottawa. Therefore, it is unlikely that Canadian governments or business would favour sharing power with it through tripartite arrangements.

Leo Panitch (1979b), the major Canadian participant in the debate, has not only confirmed all these skeptical assessments but also added that the unions themselves would probably react adversely to government-induced attempts at mutual wage restraint (incomes policy), which they would perceive as a further attempt to draw their teeth in order to stabilize the economy at the expense of the workers.

However, when all this has been said, there is no denying that the general tripartite concept of government-mediated accommodation among conflicting major interest organizations is worth exploring further, especially since certain collaborative efforts have already periodically been made. A political indication of the feasibility of such a path might be seen in the fact that the NDP survived the 1984 Conservative election victory and actually gained seats in Ontario, where the structural crisis of declining industries urgently requires some compromising restructuring formula. At the same time, it must be pointed out that all efforts at reform of Canada's institutions and processes can only be successful if they fully allow for the country's highly fragmented and regionalized socioeconomic structure.

Reform Proposals:
Consultation and Planning Mechanisms

The objectives of any reform proposals should include: (1) the avoidance of unnecessary federal-provincial confrontation, (2) the taking into account of the expertise of organized interests into the federal-provincial process of policy formation, and (3) the adoption of a formula for national economic policy making, which encourages and protects the economic union given a high degree of sectoral and regional fragmentation. Of course, these objectives are in part mutually exclusive (1 and 2) and in part asymmetrically overlapping (2 and 3). This is reflected in the main messages from the briefs presented to the Commission. Consider some of the summarized findings:

- While the business community seems to be generally in favour of minimizing government intervention, it is at the same time divided over the issue of an industrial strategy with government involvement.
- There is very little general concern with or interest in the problems of federal-provincial relations, while at the same time a substantial amount of regional loyalty persists; and there is no demand for fundamental jurisdictional change.
- Despite this persistent and not unexpected regionalism, which is reflected in parallel stances of governments, the issue of the economic union seems to divide the interest group community along nonregional cleavage lines (divisions *within* the business community, and *between* business and labour).

The prevailing message of the briefs to the Commission largely confirms what is generally known: that the Canadian socioeconomic and political fabric is so complex and "messy" that no formula for institutional tidiness could be found to enable Canada to live the life of a nation-state with a simple economic and market structure. As the briefs seem to suggest, there is a considerable element of illusion involved in Canadian discussions about the economic union, industrial restructuring and the reduction of intergovernmental conflict. What have been characterized as motherhood issues in the preceding chapter, namely the exasperation with federal-provincial fighting and an increased desire for more effective consultation between interest groups and the governments, is just such an illusion — at least when accompanied by the assumption that the one could be smoothly substituted for the other. What Canadian interest groups seem to say is: forget about these idle fights about government principles and let us get on with business. But then it is exactly this "getting on with business" in a fragmented socioeconomic system, which causes much of the federal-provincial fighting in the first place.

There is another even more problematic illusion. Many Canadians seem to think that their country is handicapped because it lacks much of the neat institutional tidiness attributed to their more successful rivals in the international market, especially West Germany and Japan. This illusion, which has at least three aspects, only leads us away from those paths to reform that could realistically be taken in this country. First, Canada is not Germany or Japan. The West German political culture is biased by a prevailing preoccupation with the avoidance of conflict. Its economy during the postwar restructuring phase was oriented overwhelmingly to exports, and this now poses structural problems requiring government-induced restraint at the cost of a growing number of increasingly marginalized groups and economic sectors no longer admitted to the mainstream of political decision making. The consequences are the formation of many protest movements and the rise of the Green Party. The introduction of such a politics of "limited pluralism" (von Beyme, 1978) would be quite unacceptable in Canada. Likewise Canadians would probably be unwilling to stomach the social costs of the Japanese "model".[5]

Second, there are many indications that the traditional institutions of the modern nation-state are growing obsolescent under the strain of economic crisis and structural fragmentation in all advanced industrial democracies. It would, therefore, be foolish and anachronistic in the Canadian context to try to pull in a direction that no longer seems to work too well elsewhere.

Third, it would be a waste of Canada's political and economic reform possibilities if the untidiness of its institutions were forcefully constrained by outdated models. The Canadian experience, with its improvised politics, in coping with the problems of fragmentation should be seen as an asset, not as a liability.

Having said that, a few reform proposals can still be offered which may help to adapt the Canadian situation to a more conscious concept of harmonization and to encompass the necessary planning of the economy. In the first place, some suggestions will be made for general improvement of the consultative mechanisms between organized interest groups and central institutions; and then a more substantial proposal will be made in the direction of a new planning agency to bring together the two sides of Canadian political life, the broad spectrum of interests, and the inevitable process of intergovernmental relations.

Strengthening Consultative Mechanisms

If there is a general statement that could subsume the most commonly expressed viewpoint of the briefs made to the Commission, surely it is: "We need more consultation with everyone, at every level, on everything and at all times."[6] Intervenors want more ready access to the decision-making process, and they want to know what is going on, what is being actively considered by government. If they were granted these, they say, they would make a more valuable contribution to the policy process, and they would come to trust government more. There is, almost by definition, truth in this general position, although one must also recognize that it amounts to a unilateral request to be granted more power and information. To grant it uncritically may amount to widening the gap between the institutionalized groups and the others (depending on what exactly was done); and it may also serve to diminish the power and discretion of the government decision makers (ministers, senior officials and Parliament both in session and in committee). What is needed, therefore, is a more systematic and institutionalized mechanism of consultation, in which all groups know how they can make their inputs, and are assured of a measure of fairness in competition with other groups. However, this must be done in a way which does not undermine the capacity of government to come to decisions in reasonable time, and in an atmosphere of impartiality and concern for the public interest.

There are really two concerns here: many groups find the methods for consultation currently employed to be partial, unpredictable and inadequate; and they complain of undue secrecy on the part of government.

To meet the former criticism there should be a study of consultation mechanisms undertaken by the legislative bodies at both levels of government with a view to putting in place a system that would be perceived as adequate and fair. Consideration might be given to the following:

First, a more regularized procedure of parliamentary committees, with more power and influence, to enable groups to know that they could be heard, and to enable them to make their representations in open sessions. Each group would know the position of the others and, therefore, could respond in public.

Second, analogous to this would be a more systematic and common use of task forces, royal commissions and cabinet committees hearing representations from interest groups, especially in open sessions. The point would be to put into effect a general institutionalized, formal mechanism for consultation, in which each group would know its rights and the position of other intervenors. On the other hand, care must be taken to avoid costly formalism, such as reliance on legal counsel to make submissions. This has already served to make the hearings of some regulatory commissions available only to wealthy and technically informed interests (and it, in turn, has led the CRTC to recommend the assessing of the costs of counsel for public interest intervenors against the licensed operator).

Third, another variant of this position is the old remedy for handling interest group representations that has been proposed by political scientists over the past two decades. It is that the government receive the representations of groups in formalized advisory boards, on which all sides of a question would be represented. The virtue of this arrangement is seen to be the building-in of a dialogue between different points of view in the open, in the presence of government representatives. Presumably, this should lead to reasonable accommodations between different points of view and should make it possible for interest groups to make certain that the government is not deceived by biased or one-sided representations from particular groups. Regulatory bodies already exist which, in a certain sense, accomplish this. The proposal then is to extend this arrangement into more general policy making areas, thereby increasing openness and publicity, and encouraging dialogue between groups in the presence of policy makers.

For example, the Canadian Radio-television and Telecommunications Commission follows a procedure regarding broadcasting applications, in which informal hearings are held. The applicants are heard and are questioned on their written and oral presentations. Then the intervenors are also heard and questioned, followed by the reply of the applicants. After this open hearing when all relevant points of view have been heard and followed up, the panel of commissioners, having studied the memoranda prepared by staff, reaches its recommendation, which goes to the full Commission (including the part-time commissioners) for consultation. The final decision is reached by the executive committee (Law Reform Commission, 1980, pp. 22–28). In short, the hearing of opinion is conducted in public, and the discussion of policy occurs in private.

These proposed remedies would probably help appease the established groups and would ensure a more systematic structure of consultation, but they would do nothing to answer the complaint of the groups that find themselves excluded, and of course the unorganized would be unaffected. Indeed, complaints of elitism and partial selectivity directed at present arrangements may apply *a fortiori* to the above proposals, unless care were taken to assure such groups of a place in the system. The rights of the unorganized can, of course, be taken account of by special "ombudsman" or other such arrangements. In the final analysis, the appearance of fairness and trust give such people good reason not to bestir themselves to become organized.

If the government is seriously concerned to see that public interest groups that lack financial means are heard, it could adopt the radical course of aiding them with funds to cover the costs of appearing. One suggestion, by Fred Thompson and W.T. Stanbury, is that "directed public funding of interest group activities, perhaps by means of an optional checkoff on the annual income tax return"[7] be adopted. This would permit citizens to support the interest group of their choice, just as they can support their chosen political party, with part of the cost deducted from tax owing to the government (Thompson and Stanbury, 1979, pp. 51–52).

Fourth, this leads to the final of these piecemeal suggestions: more openness in government, to build up trust and to inform the people. The recent freedom of information legislation enacted at both levels of government is a major factor, as far as the individual is concerned. At the more general level, trust could be earned by making public documents more available to citizens and by greater recourse to the open consultation arrangements noted above.

Disentanglement Through Changes in the Division of Power

Under the Constitution, agriculture and immigration are concurrent areas of jurisdiction between federal and provincial governments. Trade and commerce within provincial boundaries comes under provincial jurisdiction, and between provinces and with other countries it comes under federal control. The provincial governments are given taxation powers of a specific kind, whereas the federal government can impose any form of taxation. These are merely the most obvious examples of overlapping jurisdiction. If such areas of overlap were to be redefined so as to diminish these areas, presumably the possibilities of friction and conflict might be reduced. Not only would such action diminish intergovernmental contact and, therefore, the possibility for friction, but it would also tend to segregate the interest group structures of the federal government from those of the provincial governments. We require a more pragmatic approach to questions of jurisdiction, as well as greater willingness to make changes in accordance with the needs of today. Many changes have occurred in Canada since 1867, and the division of powers created then should be updated too. The governments would have to be willing to make some trade-offs in order for each to have a more self-contained and appropriate mix of powers and jurisdiction. Of course, any such redefinition of jurisdictional boundaries would require the mutual consent of both levels of government and, therefore, may be more of a chimera than a realistic solution. In any event, such action is far from likely to serve as a general remedy for the difficulties of divided jurisdiction.

The briefs to the Commission tended to agree that the division of powers is to be accepted. Canadians have lived with them for 117 years without major change (except for unemployment insurance being made a federal responsibility in 1940), so now there is a general disposition to take them as given. One national corporation (CIL) did suggest that uniform labour law across the country is necessary to avoid the confusion caused by the present situation. There was some expression of opinion in Quebec that some clarification of the division of powers is needed, through the good offices of a conciliation commission:

> . . . qui pourrait faciliter les ententes, rapprocher les deux gouvernements concernés dans le contexte de l'exercice de pouvoirs de chacun.
> (Fédération UPA Lac St-Jean, Brief, November 2, 1983, p. 10)

While it is difficult to perceive how such an institution might be set up, the function proposed could be subsumed in the federal-provincial planning secretariat proposed below.

A Federal-Provincial Planning Secretariat

Canada is facing two chronic and serious economic problems: persistent unemployment and the need to develop a productive and competitive industrial structure in order to succeed in the international marketplace. The conventional remedy for unemployment is job creation, which usually involves government funding for make-work projects. The cost of this, of course, is borne by the general taxpayer and becomes a drag on the economic viability and efficiency of the national economy, and it therefore adversely affects the country's ability to compete in international trade. In other words, the conventional remedy for the one problem becomes a means of exacerbating the other. Since there is no obvious way of escaping from the policy dilemma posed by this situation, we would be well advised to seek out improvements in our policy-making machinery in order to develop appropriate policies that are subtle and sensitive enough to meet an extremely difficult situation.

It is obvious that business, labour, voluntary groups and municipal governments all agree that there is a need for wider consultation before policy is made. However, it is equally obvious that, in a complex society, consultation on a broad scale could mean undue delay with the possibility of escalating disagreements between participants with differing points of view. There is, therefore, a need to build up machinery for effecting the desired consultation in such a way that it contributes to effective policy making. In Canada, there are two basic levels to be considered: the federal-provincial one and the one that brings together government and the private sector (business, labour and other voluntary associations). In other words, it is the two dynamics of our study — the federal-provincial one and the government-interest group one — that have to be integrated into a sound policy-making mechanism.

At the present time, no machinery has been put in place to structure the consultations between governments, on the one hand, and between government and the private sector, on the other, so as to facilitate sound policy making. It is easy to state what is needed — a means of bringing together parties with power, who represent legitimate interests in such a way that they can profit by expert opinion and be led to produce sound policy output. It is much more difficult to achieve such an objective in real life.

In the field of economic policy, both the federal government and the provincial governments have important powers and, therefore, important roles to play. The policy output of one participant affects the situation of the others. Therefore, it is obvious that there is considerable potential advantage in the coordination of policies, so that the maximum advantages for the national community as a whole can be achieved. Since governments have the power to legislate rules and enforce them, it would appear to be sensible for them to attempt to work out together some policy outputs. What we are proposing is not a Canadian version of the French indicative-planning system. Rather, it is a bringing together of effective federal and provincial policy-making authority and competent expertise oriented toward the production of integrated national economic policy. This then becomes the basic material for the business, labour and other leaders to study and work toward. The process of implementation and negotiation would be an ongoing one, sustained by the interaction of expertise and power.

Currently, Canada is relying on a somewhat ad hoc process of federal-provincial collaboration. There is considerable cooperation between line departments in the two levels of government. There has, however, been less success in aligning cooperative policies between the first ministers. Their meetings are out of the daily routine of government. They are widely publicized meetings held in part, at least, under the scrutiny of the mass media of communication. Each first minister is a kind of gladiator fighting for his community. He is under pressure not to make concessions and to achieve agreements which are demonstrably in the interest of his jurisdiction. The meetings are short and therefore do not allow for the careful study of proposals and time-consuming staff work to support the negotiations between first ministers. These are "sudden death" encounters in which a small number of men is called upon to find agreement on complex questions under conditions of pressure and strain. Better results are usually achieved when governments can work things out over longer periods of time in collaboration with their experts away from the publicity of a public conference — which creates conditions where the making of concessions becomes almost an abject act of surrender. A better solution, therefore, to the working out of overall economic policy in Canada would be through the creation of a new institution that would bring together federal and provincial representatives to work out, on an ongoing basis, economic policy arrangements in the overall national interest, which would, at the same time, take account of the needs of individual provinces. This could be accomplished by all provinces being represented. The other requirement is for an adequate input of expertise. While it is true that experts disagree with one another, their areas of disagreement are much more restricted and confined than are those of lay persons. Such a federal-provincial economic policy-making agency would require experts of two kinds: specialists in federal-provincial relations who would be attached to the new institution itself, and experts on substantive policy areas brought in by each province and the federal government in order to inform the discussions that were taking place and to work out acceptable policy compromises.

Since there are two separate functions involved, representing the different jurisdictions and providing expertise, it may be appropriate to suggest how these two functions could be combined in one body. Any federal-provincial policy-making agency would have to provide for parity of representation between the two levels of government. This suggests a board of directors drawn, say, ten from the provinces and ten from the federal government. The apportionment, of course, would be a matter of negotiation but would probably be determined on a regional basis. Federal government representation would be composed in whatever way the government chose, but it probably would draw on personnel in the economic policy-making departments of the government. This body of about twenty people would constitute the board of directors. It would have to be served by a corps of experts (the secretariat).

A key figure in the operation would be the director of the secretariat. He or she would be the chief executive officer of the professional body and the representative of it in dealing with the outside world. This representative would be in continuous liaison with the board of directors to be assured of the closest collaboration of the two bodies. Clearly, it would be essential to appoint a highly skilled person to this position, who has the confidence of the board and is respected in the private sector. This appointment is the most important single act in setting up such an arrangement. One has only to think of Jean Monnet's role in the French planning commission or, indeed, John Deutsch's in the early days of the Economic Council of Canada.

Since the secretariat would have to prepare the initial proposals, it would have to have very high quality senior staff. It would have to have freedom to consult widely. In order to provide the best bias in favour of cooperation, it would be essential that the experts be attached permanently to the institution itself, rather than simply being seconded from government departments. Its proposals would first go before the board of directors for discussion and elaboration. Presumably, they would provide the basis for cooperative arrangements between the levels of government in order to harmonize policies.

This process would merely constitute the first step. For economic development policies to be carried forward successfully, there would be need for the collaboration of the private sector. As the submissions to the Commission have shown, there is a great thirst for consultation among the various interests in the country. Since economic development plans must involve the private sector directly or indirectly, it is important to make certain that the best possible arrangements exist for maximizing cooperation.

There is a need for two things: clear leadership in elaborating plans for development and adequate consultation mechanisms in order to make certain that support from the potential participants is effectively enlisted. It is important that, when the representatives of business and labour are called upon to assist government, they are presented with more than the question: "What do you want?" If they could be presented with an outline of proposals which had been agreed to by representatives of both levels of government, they would know that careful staff work had been done and that the authority of both levels of government was committed. The program would be a serious one, which already had a substantial element of support. The representatives of labour and business would be asked for their support and collaboration, and in many cases there would be promises of government support in order to achieve the agreed upon goals. It is important that the government agency take the initiative in elaborating the general direction of policy and the overall objectives. Then there would be clarity and leadership, and the representatives of the business and labour interests would know where government stood, and they could react clearly to it. Policy would be directed to clear national goals.

This proposal, of course, is not a solution to Canada's problems. Rather, it is a suggestion for a mechanism to deal with those problems. It emphasizes clarity between the federal government and the provinces and between business and labour. This is suggested because it is difficult to imagine any one of these four elements agreeing to accept a subordinate position; what is important is that they all participate and that they feel comfortable in their roles.

Certainly, there would be various obstacles facing such a mechanism. Canada does not have national organizations to speak for either business or labour. Rather, it has a large number of bodies that are inclined to compete with one another. This has generally been considered to be an obstacle to the setting up of such an agency. It may be so. On the other hand, one must recognize that peak organizations that meet one another have that kind of diplomatic sanctity that we know so well in federal-provincial conferences. Meetings between such groups have the power to decide too much, and therefore often cannot decide anything. Certainly, Canada is spared this sort of confrontation at the private sector summit. On the other hand, it may be possible to work out arrangements among the large number of groups and organizations to put together effective representation made up of persons none of whom can be viewed as *the* representative for either of these great estates. Maybe Canadians would be more likely to find agreement if greater scope were left to specialist participants and to the larger number of people who would speak for the various organizations concerned.

As noted above, there are many conflicting interests in Canada, as indeed there are in all countries. It is difficult to work out trade-offs in all circumstances. What is suggested is a mechanism to take maximum advantage of expertise and negotiation in the best atmosphere for compromise. And if additional representative bodies have to be devised to speak for those elements that are not currently organized, so be it. Since discussion will take place anyway, it is important that it be structured so that it makes the best possible contribution to policy making and the integration of the Canadian community.

Appendix A
Briefs: Regional Breakdown (Percent)

Classified According to Submitting Organization

Type	Quantity	Atlantic	Quebec	Ontario	Prairies	B.C.	N.W.T.
All briefs	1,158	12.3	13.5	38.5	19.8	13.0	2.6
Business	297	9.8	15.5	43.8	18.2	10.1	2.4
Labour	61	19.7	16.4	37.7	11.5	11.5	3.3
Voluntary	234	12.0	12.4	38.9	18.4	15.4	3.0
Population of Canada (1983)	24,889,800	9.1	26.2	35.4	17.6	11.3	0.3

Briefs that Addressed a Specific Issue

Issue	Quantity	Atlantic	Quebec	Ontario	Prairies	B.C.	Yukon and N.W.T.
Govt. Intervention	124	7.3	18.5	41.1	20.2	12.1	0.8
Industrial Strategy	27	18.5	14.8	37.0	14.8	11.1	0
Foreign Investment	49	2.0	14.3	61.2	12.2	6.1	4.1
Consultation	72	5.6	15.3	47.2	15.3	15.3	1.4
Fed.-Prov. Relations	33	9.1	15.2	63.6	9.1	3.0	0
Division of Powers	51	13.7	9.8	51.0	19.6	5.9	0
Decentralization	18	27.8	44.4	16.7	5.6	0	5.6
Economic Union	43	7.0	16.3	58.1	14.0	4.7	0
Regional Dev. Policy	28	25.0	25.0	25.0	3.6	10.7	10.7

Appendix B
Excerpts from Briefs from the Atlantic Provinces

The Atlantic region . . . has little importance in national political terms
. . . . Atlantic Canadians have little "leverage" in political terms and thus
have limited means to influence national policy to favour the region. Relationships between the individual provincial governments and Ottawa are
of a David and Goliath nature, not only because of the relative size of
the governments but also because the small Atlantic governments cannot
afford the depth of expertise available to the senior government. This
inequality is further compounded by the fiscal realities of the relationship, since all four Atlantic provinces are heavily dependent on Ottawa
for funding through transfer payments. It is a David and Goliath scenario
complicated by the fact that David must rely on Goliath for his supper.
(Atlantic Provinces Chamber of Commerce, Brief, September 6, 1983,
pp. 3–4)

Atlantic Canada and Saint John need continued federal support, but
the proper kind of support. It needs a well conceived long-range plan of
action to enable it to develop its full potential and stand on its own
feet. . . . It is clear that a change in federal thinking and policy making
must take place. (Saint John Board of Trade, Brief, September 2, 1983,
p. 10)

For too long the Atlantic region has been a womb for industrial Canada.
We suggest a reassessment of those national policies, which artificially
support an industrial base in Central Canada. (Dartmouth Chamber of
Commerce, Brief, October 3, 1983, p. 16)

We, [in the Atlantic region] operate on about $1,600,000,000 of revenue
a year, of which half of that — $800 million — comes from the federal
government in transfer payments in one form or another. We are not happy
about that. . . . (Nova Scotia Federation of Labour Transcript, Halifax,
October, 1983 [v. 22], p. 4210)

[The Atlantic] region is not served equally with the other provinces by
the national energy policy of the federal government. (Capital Region
Development Commission Inc., New Brunswick, Brief, September 8, 1983,
p. 3)

Canada's national industrial policy has favoured Central Canada, leaving the Maritime provinces, in general, and New Brunswick, in particular,
to develop their primary resources for export markets. (New Brunswick
Liberal party, p. 10). At the time of Confederation, New Brunswick
believed strongly in the common good and sharing, a most important value
upon which Canada was founded. The creation and enforcement of a new
Canadian economic union was a vital component of the social contract
agreed to. This contract has not been kept. The expectations promised
by Confederation have not been fulfilled. We feel that New Brunswick

has been let down by Confederation. (New Brunswick Liberal Party, Brief, September 12, 1983, p. 18)

We have found in the past that Central Canada's attitude towards us and, by extension, of the federal government's attitude towards us, to be very paternalistic. This, in turn, is reflected in the political decisions, which are made affecting the Maritimes. (City of Charlottetown, Brief, September 14, 1983, p. 3)

It is becoming clear . . . that the federal government has abandoned any pretence of stimulating economic development in Atlantic Canada, or of reducing the disparity between Atlantic Canada and the rest of the country, with the dismantling of the Department of Regional Economic Expansion. (New Brunswick New Democratic Party, Brief, September 20, 1983, p. 2)

We are worse off in the Atlantic region than are those in the rest of the country. Unemployment is higher, wages are lower. We also, perhaps not surprisingly, have less control over our own resources and economy than those in the rest of the country and, as a result, also have less protection for our quality of life than do others. (Nova Scotia New Democratic Party, Brief, September 29, 1983, p. 4)

Nova Scotia has never been a full partner in Confederation. . . . Development with federal government financing has worked against us. (Nova Scotia Federation of Labour, Brief, September 6, 1983, p. 4)

We are not getting our fair share of industrial development [in the Atlantic region.] (Marine Workers' Federation, Transcript, Halifax, October 13, 1983 [v. 24], p. 4672)

We would like to say that our definition of regional disparity, which has caused a great deal of underdevelopment in this region, and which really goes back to the time of Confederation, lies in the control of resources and decision making by central Canada, which has robbed this region of some of its most dynamic resources, including people. (Social Action Commission, Roman Catholic Diocese of Charlottetown, Transcript, September 19, 1983 [v. 10], p. 2564)

Notes

CHAPTER 1

1. For an elaboration of this point, see F.R. Scott, "French Canada and Federalism," in *Evolving Canadian Federalism*, edited by A.R.M. Lower, F.R. Scott et al. (Durham, N.C.: Duke University Press, 1958), pp. 54–91.

CHAPTER 3

1. Press release of a meeting with Western news media representatives, Ottawa, July 8, 1983, pp. 14–15.
2. House of Commons, Standing Committee on Transport, Minutes and Proceedings, August 10, 1983, pp. 115A–118.
3. September 27, 1983.
4. Ibid.
5. Bill C-150, re-introduced in the 1984 session as Bill C-12.
6. *Alberta in Canada: Strength in Diversity*, a Government of Alberta Discussion Paper, 1983, p. 50.
7. Press release, Ottawa, July 8, 1983, p. 12.
8. *The Financial Post*, December 31, 1983, p. 23.
9. *Harmony in Diversity: A New Federalism for Canada*, 1978, p. 17.
10. *Edmonton Journal*, February 3, 1983, p. A2.
11. Budget, Government of Prince Edward Island, March 1983.
12. Quoted in *Maclean's*, August 15, 1983, p. 10.
13. *Alberta in Canada: Strength in Diversity*, 1983, passim.
14. *The Globe and Mail*, February 7, 1984.

CHAPTER 5

1. All provincial governments were consulted by the Commission. Some made submissions while others participated in private meetings.

CHAPTER 6

1. See Richard Simeon and David J. Elkins, *Small Worlds* (Toronto: Methuen, 1980), esp. chap. 8; Richard Simeon with E. Robert Miller, "Regional Variations in Public Policy," in *Small Worlds* (Toronto: Methuen, 1980), pp. 242–84.
2. See Stein Rokkan and Derek W. Urwin, *Economy, Territory, Identity* (London: Sage Publications, 1983), pp. 6–18, for a discussion of this point.
3. See David A. Wolfe, "The Politics of the Deficit," in *The Politics of Economic Policy*, volume 40 of the research studies prepared for the Royal Commission on the Economic Union and Development Prospects for Canada (Toronto: University of Toronto Press, 1985).
4. For a key to this literature, see *The International Political Science Review* 4, (2)(1983) — a special issue devoted to *Interest Intermediation: Toward New Corporatism(s)*, edited by Gerhard Lehmbruch and Jack Hayward. Also, see Suzanne Berger, ed., *Organizing Interests in Western Europe* (New York: Cambridge University Press, 1981); and Philippe C. Schmitter and Gerhard Lehmbruch, *Trends Toward Corporatist Intermediation* (Beverly Hills: Sage Publications, 1979); and Gerhard Lehmbruch and Philippe C. Schmitter, *Patterns of Corporatist Policy-Making* (Beverly Hills: Sage Publications, 1982).

5. See Bill Watson, "Industrial Policies: Picking Winners," *The Whig Standard Magazine*, Kingston, 18 February 1984, pp. 6–8.

6. Michelle Doray, *The Consultation Process*, a Staff Report to the Royal Commission on the Economic Union and Development Prospects for Canada, p. 1.

7. For a more detailed discussion of this proposal see H.G. Thorburn, *Planning and the Economy, Building Federal-Provincial Consensus* (Toronto: James Lorimer, 1984), pp. 210–45.

Bibliography

Armstrong, Christopher. 1981. *The Politics of Federalism: Ontario's Relations with the Federal Government, 1867–1942*. Toronto: University of Toronto Press.

Berger, Suzanne, ed. 1981. *Organizing Interests in Western Europe*. New York: Cambridge University Press.

Bernard, André. 1977. *La politique au Canada et au Québec*. 2d ed. Montreal: Les Presses de l'Université du Québec.

Bernard, L. 1979. "La conjoncture actuelle des relations intergouvernementales." In *Confrontation and Collaboration — Intergovernmental Relations in Canada Today*, edited by R. Simeon, pp. 99–104. Toronto: Institute of Public Administration of Canada.

Berry, Glyn R. 1974. "The Oil Lobby and the Energy Crisis." *Canadian Public Administration* 17.

Brown, Douglas, and Julia Eastman. 1981. *The Limits of Consultation: A Debate Among Ottawa, the Provinces and the Private Sector on an Industrial Strategy*. Study prepared for the Science Council of Canada and the Institute of Intergovernmental Relations, Queen's University. Ottawa: Minister of Supply and Services Canada.

Brunelle, Dorval. 1981. "Économie politique et rapatriement." *Les Cahiers du socialisme* 8.

Bucovetsky, M.W. 1975. "The Mining Industry and the Great Tax Reform Debate." In *Pressure Group Behaviour in Canadian Politics*, edited by A. Paul Pross. Toronto: McGraw-Hill Ryerson.

Cairns, Alan. 1977. "The Governments and Societies of Canadian Federalism." *Canadian Journal of Political Science* (December): 695–726.

———. 1979. "The Other Crisis of Canadian Federalism." *Canadian Public Administration* (Summer): 175–95.

Chandler, Martha, and William Chandler. 1979. *Public Policy and Provincial Politics*. Toronto: McGraw-Hill Ryerson.

Clement, Wallace. 1975. *The Canadian Corporate Elite*. Toronto: McClelland and Stewart.

———. 1983. *Class, Power and Property*. Toronto: Methuen.

Corry, J.A. 1958. "Constitutional Trends and Federalism." In *Evolving Canadian Federalism*, edited by A.R.M. Lower et al. Durham, N.C.: Duke University Press.

Crozier, Michel J. et al. 1975. *The Crisis of Democracy*. New York: New York University Press.

Dawson, Helen Jones. 1960. "An Interest Group: The Canadian Federation of Agriculture." *Canadian Public Administration* 3: 134–49.

———. 1963. "The Consumers' Association of Canada." *Canadian Public Administration* 6: 92–118.

———. 1975. "National Pressure Groups and the Federal Government." In *Pressure Group Behaviour in Canadian Politics*, edited by A. Paul Pross. Toronto: McGraw-Hill Ryerson.

Doerr, Audrey D. 1971. "The Role of White Papers." In *The Structure of Policy-Making in Canada*, edited by G. Bruce Doern and Peter Aucoin. Toronto: Macmillan.

———. 1982. "The Role of Coloured Papers." *Canadian Public Administration* 25 (Fall): 366–79.

Fach, Wolfgang. 1983. "Ausgangspunkt des Diskurses, Ende des Modells?" *Journal für Sozialforschung* 23, no. 3.

Faulkner, J. Hugh. 1982. "Pressuring the Executive." *Canadian Public Administration* 25 (Summer): 240–53.

Fournier, Pierre. 1978. "Le Parti Québécois et la conjoncture économique au Québec." *Politique aujourd'hui*: 7–8.

——. 1983. "The New Parameters of the Quebec Bourgeoisie." In *The Quebec State*, edited by Alain Gagnon. Toronto: Methuen.

Gillies, James. 1981. *Where Business Fails: Business-Government Relations at the Federal Level in Canada*. Montreal: Institute for Research on Public Policy.

Gillies, James, and Jean Pigott. 1982. "Participation in the Legislative Process." *Canadian Public Administration* 25 (Summer): 254–64.

Greenwald, C.S. 1977. *Group Power: Lobbying and Public Policy*. New York: Praeger.

Hosek, Chaviva. 1983. "Women and the Constitutional Process." In *And No One Cheered*, edited by K. Banting and R. Simeon. Toronto: Methuen.

Inglehart, Ronald. 1977. *The Silent Revolution*. Princeton: Princeton University Press.

Kwavnick, David. 1970. "Pressure Group Demands and the Struggle for Organizational Status: The Case of Organized Labour in Canada." *Canadian Journal of Political Science* 3: 56–72.

——. 1973. *Organized Labour and Pressure Politics*. Toronto: Macmillan.

——. 1975. "Interest Group Demands and the Federal Political System: Two Canadian Case Studies." In *Pressure Group Behaviour in Canadian Politics*, edited by A. Paul Pross. Toronto: McGraw-Hill Ryerson.

Law Reform Commission of Canada. 1980. *The Canadian Radio-television and Telecommunications Commission*. Ottawa: Minister of Supply and Services Canada.

Legaré, Anne. 1978. "Les classes sociales et le gouvernement P.Q. à Québec." *Canadian Review of Sociology and Anthropology* 15.

Lehmbruch, Gerhard. 1984. "An Interorganizational Perspective on Neocorporatism." Paper for the Workshop on Industrial Democracy, ECPR Joint Sessions, Salzburg, April 13–18.

Lehmbruch, Gerhard, and Jack Hayward, eds. 1983. *The International Political Science Review* 4 (2).

Lehmbruch, G., and Philippe C. Schmitter. 1982. *Patterns of Corporatist Policy-Making*. Beverly Hills: Sage Publications.

Levitt, Kari. 1970. *Silent Surrender*. Toronto: Macmillan.

Lowi, Theodore J. 1979. *The End of Liberalism*. 2d ed. New York: Norton.

Maxwell, J.A. 1937. *Federal Subsidies to Provincial Governments in Canada*. Cambridge, Mass.: Harvard University Press.

Nelles, H.V. 1973. *The Politics of Development*. Toronto: Macmillan.

Niosi, Jorge. 1981. *Canadian Capitalism*. Toronto: James Lorimer.

Offe, Claus. 1981. "The Attribution of Public Status to Interest Groups: Observations on the West German Case." In *Organizing Interests in Western Europe*, edited by S. Berger. New York: Cambridge University Press.

——. 1984. *Contradictions of the Welfare State*. London: Hutchinson.

Olson, M., Jr. 1968. *The Logic of Collective Action*. New York: Schocken Books.

Panitch, Leo, ed. 1977. *The Canadian State: Political Economy and Political Power*. Toronto: University of Toronto Press.

——. 1979a. "Corporatism in Canada." *Studies in Political Economy* (Spring).

——. 1979b. "Corporatism in Canada." In *The Canadian Political Process*, 3d ed., edited by R. Schultz, O.M. Kruhlak, and J.C. Terry. Toronto: Holt, Rinehart and Winston.

——. 1979c. "The Role and Nature of the Canadian State." In *The Canadian State*, edited by L. Panitch. Toronto: University of Toronto Press.

——. 1984. "Class and Power in Canada." Paper for the Association for Canadian Studies, Grainau, West Germany, February 16–19.

Pizzorno, Alessandro. 1981. "Interests and Parties in Pluralism." In *Organizing Interests in Western Europe*, edited by S. Berger. New York: Cambridge University Press.

Pollard, Bruce G. 1984. *The Year in Review 1983: Intergovernmental Relations in Canada*. Kingston: Queen's University, Institute of Intergovernmental Relations.

Pratt, Larry. 1977. "The State and Province-Building." In *The Canadian State: Political Economic and Political Power*, edited by Leo Panitch. Toronto: University of Toronto Press.

Pratt, Larry, and John Richards. 1979. *Prairie Capitalism: Power and Influence in the New West*. Toronto: McClelland and Stewart.

Presthus, Robert. 1971. "Interest Groups and the Canadian Parliament: Activities, Interaction, Legitimacy and Influence." *Canadian Journal of Political Science* 4: 444–60.

—. 1974. *Elites in the Policy Process*. New York. Macmillan.

—. 1975. *Elite Accommodation in Canadian Politics*. Toronto: Macmillan.

Pross, A. Paul. 1975a. "Canadian Pressure Groups in the 1970s: Their Role and Their Relations with the Public Service." *Canadian Public Administration* 18: 121–35.

—. 1975b. "Pressure Groups: Adaptive Instruments of Political Communication." In *Pressure Group Behaviour in Canadian Politics*, edited by A. Paul Pross. Toronto: McGraw-Hill Ryerson.

—. 1976. "Pressure Groups." In *The Provincial Political Systems*, edited by David J. Bellamy, Jon H. Pammett, and Donald C. Rowat. Toronto: Methuen.

—. 1982. "Governing Under Pressure: The Special Interest Groups." *Canadian Public Administration* (Summer).

Rokkan, Stein, and Derek W. Urwin. 1983. *Economy, Territory, Identity*. London: Sage Publications.

Sanders, Douglas. 1983. "The Indian Lobby." In *And No One Cheered*, edited by K. Banting and R. Simeon. Toronto: Methuen.

Schmitter, Philippe C. 1981. "Interest Intermediation and Regime Governability in Contemporary Western Europe and North America." In *Organizing Interests in Western Europe*, edited by S. Berger. New York: Cambridge University Press.

Schmitter, Philippe C., and Gerhard Lehmbruch. 1979. *Trends Toward Corporatist Intermediation*. Beverly Hills: Sage Publications.

Schultz, Richard. 1977. "Interest Groups and Intergovernmental Negotiation: Caught in the Vise of Federalism." In *Canadian Federalism: Myth or Reality*. 3d ed., edited by Peter Meekison. Toronto: Methuen.

—. 1980. *Federalism, Bureaucracy, and Public Policy: The Politics of Highway Transport Regulation*. The Institute of Public Administration of Canada. Montreal: McGill-Queen's University Press.

Schwartz, Mildred. 1978. "The Group Basis of Politics." In *Approaches to Canadian Politics*, edited by John Redekop. Scarborough: Prentice-Hall.

Scott, F.R. 1958. "French Canada and Federalism." In *Evolving Canadian Federalism*, edited by A.R.M. Lower et al. Durham, N.C.: Duke University Press.

Simeon, Richard. 1972. *Federal-Provincial Diplomacy, The Making of Recent Policy in Canada*. Toronto: University of Toronto Press.

—. ed. 1979a. *Confrontation and Collaboration: Intergovernmental Relations in Canada Today*. Toronto: Institute of Public Administration of Canada.

—. 1979b. *Intergovernmental Relations and the Challenges to Canadian Federalism*. Kingston: Queen's University, Institute for Intergovernmental Relations.

—. 1982. "Fiscal Federalism in Canada: A Review Essay." *Canadian Tax Journal* 30 (January/February): 41–51.

Simeon, Richard, and Shelagh Dunn. 1982. "Alternative Perspectives." In *Politics of Fiscal Federalism*. Study prepared for the Economic Council of Canada. Ottawa: Minister of Supply and Services Canada.

Simeon, Richard, and David Elkins. 1980. *Small Worlds, Provinces and Parties in Canadian Political Life*. Toronto: Methuen.

Simeon, Richard, with E. Robert Miller. 1980. "Regional Variations in Public Policies." In *Small Worlds, Provinces and Parties in Canadian Political Life*, edited by R. Simeon and D. Elkins, pp. 242–84. Toronto: Methuen.

Smiley, Donald V. 1970. "Constitutional Adaptation and Canadian Federalism Since 1945." *Documents of the Royal Commission on Bilingualism and Biculturalism*. Ottawa: Queen's Printer.

——. 1980. *Canada in Question: Federalism in the Seventies*. 3d. ed. Toronto: McGraw-Hill Ryerson.

Stanbury, W.T. 1977. *Business Interests and the Reform of Canadian Competition Policy, 1971–1975*. Toronto: Carswell-Methuen.

Stevenson, Garth. 1982. *Unfulfilled Union*. Toronto: Macmillan.

Thompson, Fred, and W.T. Stanbury. 1979. *The Political Economy of Interest Groups in the Legislative Process in Canada*. Montreal: Institute for Research on Public Policy.

Thorburn, H.G. 1964. "Pressure Groups in Canadian Politics: Recent Revisions of the Anti-Combines Legislation." *Canadian Journal of Economics and Political Science* 30: 157–74.

——. 1978. "Canadian Pluralist Democracy in Crisis." *Canadian Journal of Political Science* 11 (December): 723–38.

——. 1984. *Planning and the Economy: Building Federal-Provincial Consensus*. Toronto: James Lorimer.

Truman, David. 1951. *The Governmental Process*. New York: Knopf.

Tupper, Allan. 1983. *Bill S-31 and the Federalism of State Capitalism*. Kingston: Queen's University, Institute of Intergovernmental Relations.

Veilleux, Gérard. 1979. "Evolution des mécanismes de liaison intergouvernementale." *In Confrontation and Collaboration: Intergovernmental Relations in Canada Today*, edited by Richard Simeon. Toronto: Institute of Public Administration of Canada.

von Beyme, Klaus. 1978. "The Politics of Limited Pluralism? The Case of West Germany." *Government and Opposition* 13 (3): 265–87.

Wolfe, David A. 1985. "The Politics of the Deficit." In *The Politics of Economic Policy*, volume 40 of the research studies prepared for the Royal Commission on the Economic Union and Development Prospects for Canada. Toronto: University of Toronto Press.

Ziegler, H. 1972. *Interest Groups in American Society*. 2d ed. Englewood Cliffs, N.J.: Prentice-Hall.

Zukowsky, Ronald. n.d. *Interest Groups and the Federal System in Canada*. Kingston: Queen's University, Institute of Intergovernmental Relations.

THE COLLECTED RESEARCH STUDIES

Royal Commission on the Economic Union and Development Prospects for Canada

ECONOMICS

Income Distribution and Economic Security in Canada (Vol.1), *François Vaillancourt, Research Coordinator*

Vol. 1   Income Distribution and Economic Security in Canada, *F. Vaillancourt* (C)*

Industrial Structure (Vols. 2-8), *Donald G. McFetridge, Research Coordinator*

Vol. 2   Canadian Industry in Transition, *D.G. McFetridge* (C)
Vol. 3   Technological Change in Canadian Industry, *D.G. McFetridge* (C)
Vol. 4   Canadian Industrial Policy in Action, *D.G. McFetridge* (C)
Vol. 5   Economics of Industrial Policy and Strategy, *D.G. McFetridge* (C)
Vol. 6   The Role of Scale in Canada–US Productivity Differences, *J.R. Baldwin and P.K. Gorecki* (M)
Vol. 7   Competition Policy and Vertical Exchange, *F. Mathewson and R. Winter* (M)
Vol. 8   The Political Economy of Economic Adjustment, *M. Trebilcock* (M)

International Trade (Vols. 9-14), *John Whalley, Research Coordinator*

Vol. 9   Canadian Trade Policies and the World Economy, *J. Whalley with C. Hamilton and R. Hill* (M)
Vol. 10 Canada and the Multilateral Trading System, *J. Whalley* (M)
Vol. 11 Canada–United States Free Trade, *J. Whalley* (C)
Vol. 12 Domestic Policies and the International Economic Environment, *J. Whalley* (C)
Vol. 13 Trade, Industrial Policy and International Competition, *R. Harris* (M)
Vol. 14 Canada's Resource Industries and Water Export Policy, *J. Whalley* (C)

Labour Markets and Labour Relations (Vols. 15-18), *Craig Riddell, Research Coordinator*

Vol. 15 Labour-Management Cooperation in Canada, *C. Riddell* (C)
Vol. 16 Canadian Labour Relations, *C. Riddell* (C)
Vol. 17 Work and Pay: The Canadian Labour Market, *C. Riddell* (C)
Vol. 18 Adapting to Change: Labour Market Adjustment in Canada, *C. Riddell* (C)

Macroeconomics (Vols. 19-25), *John Sargent, Research Coordinator*

Vol. 19 Macroeconomic Performance and Policy Issues: Overviews, *J. Sargent* (M)
Vol. 20 Post-War Macroeconomic Developments, *J. Sargent* (C)
Vol. 21 Fiscal and Monetary Policy, *J. Sargent* (C)
Vol. 22 Economic Growth: Prospects and Determinants, *J. Sargent* (C)
Vol. 23 Long-Term Economic Prospects for Canada: A Symposium, *J. Sargent* (C)
Vol. 24 Foreign Macroeconomic Experience: A Symposium, *J. Sargent* (C)
Vol. 25 Dealing with Inflation and Unemployment in Canada, *C. Riddell* (M)

Economic Ideas and Social Issues (Vols. 26 and 27), *David Laidler, Research Coordinator*

Vol. 26 Approaches to Economic Well-Being, *D. Laidler* (C)
Vol. 27 Responses to Economic Change, *D. Laidler* (C)

* (C) denotes a Collection of studies by various authors coordinated by the person named.
  (M) denotes a Monograph.

POLITICS AND INSTITUTIONS OF GOVERNMENT

Canada and the International Political Economy (Vols. 28-30), *Denis Stairs and Gilbert R. Winham, Research Coordinators*

Vol. 28 Canada and the International Political/Economic Environment, *D. Stairs and G.R. Winham* (C)
Vol. 29 The Politics of Canada's Economic Relationship with the United States, *D. Stairs and G.R. Winham* (C)
Vol. 30 Selected Problems in Formulating Foreign Economic Policy, *D. Stairs and G.R. Winham* (C)

State and Society in the Modern Era (Vols. 31 and 32), *Keith Banting, Research Coordinator*

Vol. 31 State and Society: Canada in Comparative Perspective, *K. Banting* (C)
Vol. 32 The State and Economic Interests, *K. Banting* (C)

Constitutionalism, Citizenship and Society (Vols. 33-35), *Alan Cairns and Cynthia Williams, Research Coordinators*

Vol. 33 Constitutionalism, Citizenship and Society in Canada, *A. Cairns and C. Williams* (C)
Vol. 34 The Politics of Gender, Ethnicity and Language in Canada, *A. Cairns and C. Williams* (C)
Vol. 35 Public Opinion and Public Policy in Canada, *R. Johnston* (M)

Representative Institutions (Vols. 36-39), *Peter Aucoin, Research Coordinator*

Vol. 36 Party Government and Regional Representation in Canada, *P. Aucoin* (C)
Vol. 37 Regional Responsiveness and the National Administrative State, *P. Aucoin* (C)
Vol. 38 Institutional Reforms for Representative Government, *P. Aucoin* (C)
Vol. 39 Intrastate Federalism in Canada, *D.V. Smiley and R.L. Watts* (M)

The Politics of Economic Policy (Vols. 40-43), *G. Bruce Doern, Research Coordinator*

Vol. 40 The Politics of Economic Policy, *G.B. Doern* (C)
Vol. 41 Federal and Provincial Budgeting, *A.M. Maslove, M.J. Prince and G.B. Doern* (M)
Vol. 42 Economic Regulation and the Federal System, *R. Schultz and A. Alexandroff* (M)
Vol. 43 Bureaucracy in Canada: Control and Reform, *S.L. Sutherland and G.B. Doern* (M)

Industrial Policy (Vols. 44 and 45), *André Blais, Research Coordinator*

Vol. 44 Canadian Industrial Policy, *A. Blais* (C)
Vol. 45 The Political Sociology of Industrial Policy, *A. Blais* (M)

LAW AND CONSTITUTIONAL ISSUES

Law, Society and the Economy (Vols. 46-51), *Ivan Bernier and Andrée Lajoie, Research Coordinators*

Vol. 46 Law, Society and the Economy, *I. Bernier and A. Lajoie* (C)
Vol. 47 The Supreme Court of Canada as an Instrument of Political Change, *I. Bernier and A. Lajoie* (C)
Vol. 48 Regulations, Crown Corporations and Administrative Tribunals, *I. Bernier and A. Lajoie* (C)
Vol. 49 Family Law and Social Welfare Legislation in Canada, *I. Bernier and A. Lajoie* (C)
Vol. 50 Consumer Protection, Environmental Law and Corporate Power, *I. Bernier and A. Lajoie* (C)
Vol. 51 Labour Law and Urban Law in Canada, *I. Bernier and A. Lajoie* (C)

The International Legal Environment (Vols. 52-54), *John Quinn, Research Coordinator*

Vol. 52 The International Legal Environment, *J. Quinn* (C)
Vol. 53 Canadian Economic Development and the International Trading System, *M.M. Hart* (M)
Vol. 54 Canada and the New International Law of the Sea, *D.M. Johnston* (M)

Harmonization of Laws in Canada (Vols. 55 and 56), *Ronald C.C. Cuming, Research Coordinator*

Vol. 55 Perspectives on the Harmonization of Law in Canada, *R. Cuming* (C)
Vol. 56 Harmonization of Business Law in Canada, *R. Cuming* (C)

Institutional and Constitutional Arrangements (Vols. 57 and 58), *Clare F. Beckton and A. Wayne MacKay, Research Coordinators*

Vol. 57 Recurring Issues in Canadian Federalism, *C.F. Beckton and A.W. MacKay* (C)
Vol. 58 The Courts and The Charter, *C.F. Beckton and A.W. MacKay* (C)

FEDERALISM AND THE ECONOMIC UNION

Federalism and The Economic Union (Vols. 58-72), *Mark Krasnick, Kenneth Norrie and Richard Simeon, Research Coordinators*

Vol. 59 Federalism and Economic Union in Canada, *K. Norrie, R. Simeon and M. Krasnick* (M)
Vol. 60 Perspectives on the Canadian Economic Union, *M. Krasnick* (C)
Vol. 61 Division of Powers and Public Policy, *R. Simeon* (C)
Vol. 62 Case Studies in the Division of Powers, *M. Krasnick* (C)
Vol. 63 Intergovernmental Relations, *R. Simeon* (C)
Vol. 64 Disparities and Interregional Adjustment, *K. Norrie* (C)
Vol. 65 Fiscal Federalism, *M. Krasnick* (C)
Vol. 66 Mobility of Capital in the Canadian Economic Union, *N. Roy* (M)
Vol. 67 Economic Management and the Division of Powers, *T.J. Courchene* (M)
Vol. 68 Regional Aspects of Confederation, *J. Whalley* (M)
Vol. 69 Interest Groups in the Canadian Federal System, *H.G. Thorburn* (M)
Vol. 70 Canada and Quebec, Past and Future: An Essay, *D. Latouche* (M)
Vol. 71 The Political Economy of Canadian Federalism: 1940–1984, *R. Simeon* (M)

THE NORTH

Vol. 72 The North, *Michael S. Whittington, Coordinator* (C)

COMMISSION ORGANIZATION

Chairman
Donald S. Macdonald

Commissioners

Clarence L. Barber	William M. Hamilton	Daryl K. Seaman
Albert Breton	John R. Messer	Thomas K. Shoyama
M. Angela Cantwell Peters	Laurent Picard	Jean Casselman-Wadds
E. Gérard Docquier	Michel Robert	Catherine T. Wallace

Senior Officers

Executive Director
J. Gerald Godsoe

Director of Policy	*Senior Advisors*	*Directors of Research*
Alan Nymark	David Ablett	Ivan Bernier
	Victor Clarke	Alan Cairns
Secretary	Carl Goldenberg	David C. Smith
Michel Rochon	Harry Stewart	
Director of Administration	*Director of Publishing*	*Co-Directors of Research*
Sheila-Marie Cook	Ed Matheson	Kenneth Norrie
		John Sargent

Research Program Organization

Economics	Politics and the Institutions of Government	Law and Constitutional Issues
Research Director	*Research Director*	*Research Director*
David C. Smith	Alan Cairns	Ivan Bernier
Executive Assistant & Assistant Director (Research Services)	*Executive Assistant*	*Executive Assistant & Research Program Administrator*
I. Lilla Connidis	Karen Jackson	Jacques J.M. Shore
Coordinators	*Coordinators*	*Coordinators*
David Laidler	Peter Aucoin	Clare F. Beckton
Donald G. McFetridge	Keith Banting	Ronald C.C. Cuming
Kenneth Norrie*	André Blais	Mark Krasnick
Craig Riddell	Bruce Doern	Andrée Lajoie
John Sargent*	Richard Simeon	A. Wayne MacKay
François Vaillancourt	Denis Stairs	John J. Quinn
John Whalley	Cynthia Williams	
	Gilbert R. Winham	
Research Analysts	*Research Analysts*	*Administrative and Research Assistant*
Caroline Digby	Claude Desranleau	Nicolas Roy
Mireille Ethier	Ian Robinson	
Judith Gold		*Research Analyst*
Douglas S. Green	*Office Administration*	Nola Silzer
Colleen Hamilton	Donna Stebbing	
Roderick Hill		
Joyce Martin		

*Kenneth Norrie and John Sargent co-directed the final phase of Economics Research with David Smith